EUTHANASIA

SEVEN QUESTIONS ABOUT

VOLUNTARY ASSISTED DYING

Euthanasia: Seven Questions about Voluntary Assisted Dying

Peter Kurti

Published by Connor Court Publishing Pty Ltd, 2022.

Copyright © Peter Kurti

ALL RIGHTS RESERVED. This book contains material protected under International and Federal Copyright Laws and Treaties. Any unauthorised reprint or use of this material is prohibited. No part of this book may be reproduced or transmitted in any form or by any means, electronic or mechanical, including photocopying, recording, or by any information storage and retrieval system without express written permission from the publisher.

PO Box 7257
Redland Bay QLD 4165
sales@connorcourt.com
www.connorcourt.com

ISBN: 9781922449115

Cover design by Maria Giordano.

Picture: Anonymous Flemish master, Young woman on her deathbed circa 1621, Wikipedia Commons.

Printed in Australia.

EUTHANASIA
SEVEN QUESTIONS ABOUT VOLUNTARY ASSISTED DYING

Peter Kurti

Connor Court Publishing

For James Harlow Brown

CONTENTS

FOREWORD   Professor Patrick Parkinson AM   ix

On making death the expression of individual preference   1

Suicide in Australia: a national tragedy   13

Question 1: Where in Australia is assisted suicide legal?   17

Question 2: What does 'dying with dignity mean'?   29

Question 3: Does personal autonomy justify legalizing assisted suicide?   41

Question 4: Why do claims to a 'right to die' threaten the common good?   47

Question 5: Why should the state prevent me from ending my own life?   55

Question 6: Why are fears about descending the 'slippery slope' justified?   63

Question 7: What impact will legalised assisted suicide have on the medical profession?   75

Threescore years and ten: Standing firm against autonomy absolutists   81

Acknowledgements   87

References   89

FOREWORD

Professor Patrick Parkinson, AM

Professor of Law

The University of Queensland

We live in an age of the individual. Slowly but surely, all constraints upon individual autonomy have been challenged. Law reform to remove those constraints is promoted in the name of individual liberty or, more potently, claims of "human rights".

We have seen this, for example, in terms of sexual ethics and family life. Why should it be unlawful to commit adultery? Why should the law require a person to remain in a marriage in which, for whatever reason, he or she is unhappy or feels unfulfilled? We have seen it also in matters of life and death. Why should there be any constraints upon a woman's right to have an abortion? Why should not IVF be available to any single woman who wants to have a child? Why should there be restrictions on the right of any couple, whether heterosexual or same-sex, to commission a surrogate to carry a child whether the surrogate be a well-advised woman from the United States or an illiterate woman from rural Nepal? And in America, why should the government restrict my right to have weapons, some of which may be capable of killing hundreds of people within minutes?

As these examples show, claims of right are not confined to consensual acts or behaviours that have no impact upon the lives of others, nor to those where there are no negative societal consequences. Claims of autonomy are made notwithstanding the potential for harm to others, the cost of societal insurance for individual choices through the health and welfare systems, or the risk of exploitation of the vulnerable.

A review of recent history in Western democracies shows how quickly a society can move from saying that something is wrong (but should not be unlawful) to saying that because it is not unlawful, it is not wrong. That has been so, for example, in terms of sexual ethics, where moral prohibitions against sex before or outside of marriage, some of which were buttressed by legal consequences, have given way to a view that all consensual sex is morally neutral. To suggest that hook-ups between strangers may be morally wrong because of the harm that it can cause is to judge another's freedom of choice oppressively.

The demand for autonomy and, more than this, the demand that you will not judge my choices or constrain my desires, has now been extended into the current debate about euthanasia. As Peter Kurti demonstrates in this very helpful work, at the heart of claims to a right to die by means of assisted suicide is a claim to personal autonomy. Like so many claims before it, the right is initially presented as an exceptional one, hemmed in by limitations and surrounded by safeguards. Peter Kurti identifies the restrictions, included in the relatively new legislation enacted in Australia that allows for euthanasia to try to ensure that assisted suicide will be rare and that informed consent of a mentally well patient is always ensured.

However, we must learn the lessons of history. The right to abortion was originally confined in many countries to grave circumstances justifying the termination. It involved stringent scrutiny by medical professionals. In England, for example, the *Abortion Act 1967* (UK) effectively created an exception to the *Infant Life Preservation Act 1929* (UK) by allowing an abortion if two medical practitioners certified that the risk of injury to the physical or mental health of the pregnant woman would be greater were the pregnancy to be continued than if the pregnancy were terminated. Such restrictions, even if they were intended to ensure that abortion is "safe, legal and rare" (as Hillary Clinton once said), diminished in efficacy over time through liberal interpretation of the statutory test and lack of enforcement of the law. Over time, abortion by way of exception has tended to become abortion on demand, at least in the earlier stages of pregnancy.

Carefully controlled exceptions to a general rule become more and more ineffective through a variety of means. The first is definition inflation. The meaning of terms in the legislation, while remaining unchanged over time, becomes subject to more and more elastic interpretation.

When, for example, is suffering "unbearable"? Is that an objective test or a subjective one? If I state that my pain is unbearable, should it matter that you think it is not? Or that a great many others have, throughout history, borne much higher levels of pain with resilience and fortitude?

Another reason why normalisation occurs is because at least some medical practitioners become more and more used to signing off on the patient's wishes, believing that this ought to be the true test of whether assisted suicide should be lawful.

A third reason is lack of enforcement of the law. Even if the safeguards written into legislation are carefully drafted, they become effectively redundant if the prosecuting authorities decline ever to prosecute. So it has been with even recently passed laws prohibiting commercial surrogacy, amongst many other examples. Official records of assisted suicide, which may demonstrate adherence to the law, are most unlikely to capture practices of assisted suicide that the law, properly construed, does not condone.

As Peter Kurti explains, if individual autonomy is the justification for obtaining assistance in dying, then all requests from competent individuals ought to be honoured. Furthermore, so the argument is likely to run eventually, the law should not discriminate against mentally ill people by denying to them the right to choose an assisted death, provided they have sufficient reasoning capacity to give a legally valid consent.

Suicide is a tragedy, not a right. Yes, an individual is

free to commit suicide, as Kurti says, but to get the state involved in facilitating it through, for example, authorising the doctors to provide assistance, and pharmacists to dispense life-ending drugs, is to alter fundamentally the moral landscape. There is a slippery slope involved in reforms of this kind. We must do all we can to assist people to die with dignity, without providing them the means with which to end their lives other than through natural causes.

November 2021

On making death the expression of individual preference

> *When society has lost its moral compass, its own uncertainty inspires in it a kind of indulgence of immoral acts which is involuntarily expressed whenever they are mentioned and which makes their immorality less appreciable.*[1]

By late 2021, New South Wales (NSW) was the only Australian state not to have legalised euthanasia. Hopes that NSW would soon fall into line were high amongst advocates of physician-assisted suicide – or 'voluntary assisted dying' (VAD) as they prefer to call it. In 2017, a previous attempt to legalise euthanasia in NSW failed by one vote. Success this time around was widely, if cautiously, expected.

In October 2021, state Independent MLA, Alex Greenwich, introduced his *Voluntary Assisted Dying Bill 2021* to the State Parliament amidst a well-organised campaign of support from groups such as Go Gentle Australia, a health promotion charity, and Dying with Dignity NSW, an organisation calling for "enhanced choice at the end of life".

By evoking the spectre of unendurable suffering and torment at the end of life, supporters of the bill were, with some hesitation, optimistic that the parliament of the nation's oldest State would relent and fall into line with the rest of the country. But the thing was not quite in the bag.

Although introduced in the Legislative Assembly (lower house) the bill was quickly referred to a committee of the Legislative Council (upper house) which intends to report at the start of the new parliamentary session in 2022. While the Greenwich bill is to be debated in the Legislative Assembly in late November 2021, it will not edge any closer to the statute book until next year.

Backers of the Greenwich bill, who hoped for its quick passage into law, were disappointed. They believe there is popular support for changing the law; and, indeed, such support for euthanasia does appear to be high throughout the country.

In November 2017, Roy Morgan polled opinion about appropriate treatment to be given a "hopelessly ill patient experiencing unrelievable suffering" who had "no chance of recovering". Respondents were asked whether or not a doctor in that situation should be allowed to give a lethal dose if the patient asks for it. In 2017, 87 per cent of respondents thought the patient should be allowed to die; only 10 per cent favoured keeping the patient alive.

There has been a significant shift in support for euthanasia since Roy Morgan first posed the question in 1946. In a poll conducted that year, asking the same question concerning a "hopelessly ill patient" who is "experiencing unrelievable suffering", Roy Morgan found that the margin between the two positions was much closer: 42 per cent of respondents favoured allowing the patient to die as opposed to 41 per cent who favoured keeping the patient alive.[2]

Advocates of euthanasia invariably adopt two broad strategies in their quest to change the law. First, they appeal to popular opinion gauged on the basis of successive opinion polls that appear to indicate a surge in support for euthanasia. Accuracy of opinion polling is, however, very influenced by the way pollsters frame the questions are asked. And even if changing the law to permit doctors to kill their patients is popular with the public, a popular policy is not necessarily the *best* policy for a society and nation.

"Just because a majority votes for something does not necessarily mean that it is ethical," observes Professor Margaret Somerville, a bioethicist and legal scholar[3]. "Democracy and ethics can diverge. Likewise, just because something is legal does not necessarily mean that it is ethical."[4]

The second strategy adopted by euthanasia advocates is to frame their argument for changing the law in terms of unrelievable suffering. They like to present VAD as something like the "medical treatment of last resort", to be used only when every other option has been exhausted.

One element of this second strategy is to argue that only a

very small number of patients would ever avail themselves of this "treatment", that the circumstances would have to be quite exceptional, and that safeguards built into a VAD scheme would ensure that availability of physician-assisted suicide would be tightly controlled.

Another element is to play on fear and to emphasise what Mr Greenwich, in his second reading speech, referred to as "people's cruel pain".[5] Gruesome accounts of suffering when a patient has apparently reached the point of untreatable pain are presented in such a way as to suggest that only a most inhumane and callous person could possibly be opposed to euthanasia.

But while it is certainly true that death marks the end of every form of human experience, making it lawful for doctors to kill patients can hardly be considered an acceptable or humane form of pain palliation for a person, no matter how many safeguards against abuse are provided for in legislation.

Schemes for legalising physician-assisted suicide purport to address the problem of "unrelievable pain" caused by terminal illness. However, one of the dangers such laws present — and one vigorously denied by VAD advocates — is that the measure of "unrelievable pain" is, in the end, totally subjective. And once it includes *physical* pain, there is no reason it cannot eventually include *mental* pain.

Whilst not legally accepted at the moment in Australia, mental pain is almost certain to be included in VAD schemes as categories of eligibility expand in the future.

Indeed, there is already mounting support for legalising physician-assisted suicide in cases where the patient is not "hopelessly ill" but simply fed up with living – a feeling or attitude that is not too hard to cast as "mental pain". This was the case with Dr David Goodall, a 104-year old academic from Perth, who flew to a clinic in Basel in Switzerland in May 2018 and committed suicide with the assistance of medical staff.

Goodall's case was unusual because, while enthusiastic about accepting assistance to end his life, he met none of the qualifications normally associated with assisted suicide. As the Roy Morgan polls suggest, much of the public support for assisted suicide comes from those who think that no one should have to endure a long and painful death. But Goodall was not suffering from any terminal illness and enjoyed good general health; he was just old and frail, no longer enjoying life, and keen to die. So, he booked a flight to Switzerland.[6]

Once doctors in Basel had confirmed Dr Goodall's intention to commit suicide, and that he was of sound mind – as required under Swiss law – a lethal dose of the barbiturate, Nembutal, was prepared. By turning a wheel on a device, Dr Goodall then introduced the drug through a cannula in his arm and died soon after. Dr Goodall's supporters applauded him for having taken charge of his own death.[7]

"David is the first person I know of who fits the requirement of old age. It's a unique situation," said Dr Philip Nitschke[8], founder of Exit International, a euthanasia advocacy group. "You've got a situation where a person is simply trying to exercise what they see as an absolute right to be able to put an end to their life."[9]

This commitment to an "absolute right" to determine the time and manner of one's death is one of Exit International's key principles. Exit International also promotes the primacy of choice by maintaining a steady challenge to the idea that the only circumstances in which a person might voluntarily wish to end their own life are those of a grave and terminal illness which blights that person's life with "unrelievable pain".

What Nitschke advocates in support of Goodall and others is not release from a lingering, painful death, but a state-supported right to die at any age and for any reason.[10] Nor does Exit International think the exercise of that right should be restricted to those able to endure a long and expensive international flight. Following Goodall's death, Exit International's publication, *e-Deliverance*, commented:

> David Goodall's death has changed how assisted dying in Switzerland is viewed. Even the Swiss Medical Association has acknowledged that allowance must be made for those in extreme old age. Assisted dying is not only for people who are seriously ill. Since David's death, Exit has been receiving requests for assistance from people around the world who see Switzerland as a viable end choice.[11]

And if Switzerland is a "viable end choice", why should not

Australia be one, too? Proponents of assisted suicide lay claim to a "right to die" and demand that the state uphold this right. But the "right to die" is a false right; it is merely a rhetorical device intended to halt any further discussion about the acceptability of self-inflicted death.

Taboos surrounding suicide are weakening and it is no longer socially unacceptable to take one's own life. Use of the phrase, the "right to die", serves only to weaken that taboo further. The so-called "right" is, in other words, a myth; and those who propound it are posing a threat to the health of our culture.

One reason for the growing popularity of assisted suicide is that advocates, such as Andrew Denton[12], have successfully convinced many that the only significant objections are based on religious belief, and thus easily dismissed. Such objections, according to Denton, are nothing more than a minority view being imposed on the (non-religious) rest of us.

Denton is wrong on two counts. He is wrong in the first instance in his claim that many cogent objections to assisted suicide depend on religious arguments. They do not. Moreover, if it *were* true that the only objections to assisted suicide are based on religion, there would be little to warrant imposing such a prohibition on those outside the communities of faith.

In any case, the returns from the 2016 census conducted by the Australian Bureau of Statistics (ABS) clearly indicate that it is *non-religious* Australians who remain in the minority, notwithstanding that the number of those claiming no religious affiliation does continue to increase. In the 2016 census, the percentage of Australians reporting "No religion" had risen from 25.3 per cent in 2011 to 30.1 per cent.[13]

The topic of euthanasia and assisted suicide is one of tremendous importance for our society and culture. It calls into question fundamental beliefs about the nature of human life and well-being, and challenges some of our foundational legal, moral and cultural philosophies concerning the deliberate taking of another human life and the impact of doing so on the wider community.

It is also a very complex question calling for detailed consideration of many concepts in law, ethics, and medicine.

Euthanasia is a topic which provokes great passion and emotion amongst both proponents and opponents. It raises a very wide range of issues, and this short book can hope to do little more than address a number of the more significant ones.

It is intended as a primer on euthanasia, setting out key matters to be addressed and the nature of the threat to society posed by its legalisation. It will examine the issue of assisted suicide and euthanasia in terms of seven questions. It will show how arguments in favour of assisted suicide – often deeply dependent on human experiences of genuine misery, suffering, and sadness – are frequently persuasive simply because of their appeal to emotion.

The book will contend that when a society legitimises the deliberate killing of one human being by – or with the assistance of – another, the dignity of all human beings is diminished.

Apart from Question One, about the current legal situation in Australia concerning assisted suicide, the various questions may be read in any order. No response presupposes that other responses have been read although necessarily each response touches on matters covered elsewhere.

Some topics, such as *autonomy*, are considered in a number of responses; in order to avoid repetition, however, analyses elsewhere will not be summarised each time the topic arises. Only the aspect of the topic relevant to the particular question will be discussed in each response.

Before embarking on the enquiry, it is important to clarify the meaning of some of the key terms used in debate about assisted suicide. Language is often made to adapt as circumstances change, and terms can both fall into and out of favour.

Consistency is important, however, and is vital for keeping the lines of argument clear. A number of terms and phrases will be used in the course of answering the seven questions, but it will be helpful to define the key terms at the outset.[14]

The *Oxford English Dictionary* defines "euthanasia" as "a gentle and easy death". More recently, the word has come to mean, "the action of inducing a gentle and easy death".[15]

Some argue that doctors already often practice a discreet

form of euthanasia by using techniques of palliative care to relieve suffering.

There is, however, a world of difference between an analgesic dose and a lethal dose of a drug. It is one thing if pain reduction has the unintended effect of shortening life, but quite another if a medicine is administered with the direct object of killing the patient.

When one person deliberately kills another because that person's life is considered not to be worth living, the action is **euthanasia**. Euthanasia is **voluntary** when it is carried out with the explicit consent of the person; it is **non-voluntary** where consent has not been given for reasons such as lack of competence on the part of the person to be killed. **Involuntary** euthanasia is an act of killing that goes against the express wishes of the person to be killed.

Suicide is the act of killing oneself by whatever means. Where, as in the case of David Goodall, the act of killing is performed by the one to be killed but help is provided by another person – such as instructions on how to commit suicide or the means with which to do it – the act of killing is **assisted suicide**. Where the assistance is provided by a doctor, the act is **physician-assisted suicide**. Proponents of physician-assisted suicide now prefer to designate the process of as **voluntary assisted dying**.

While the terms **assisted suicide** and **euthanasia** are closely linked and frequently discussed together, it is not correct to use them interchangeably. In assisted suicide, the individual kills him or herself with assistance; in euthanasia, the individual is killed by another person. The distinction is important: it does not turn on whether or not the individual who dies or wishes to die has given their full, informed consent; it turns on who does the killing.

In the argument that follows – particularly in consideration of the slippery slope argument in Question Six – the two terms will, at times, be used together. This is not to conflate them but to recognise that the line between *assisting* another to kill themselves and actually *killing* another may be crossed quite easily.

Since few would wish a painful or distressing death upon another, etymology does not move the argument along very far in terms of evaluating the morality of euthanasia. It is clear, however, that administration of **non-voluntary euthanasia** (that is, where a person is put to death painlessly but without their consent) amounts to murder.

It is thus more helpful to focus attention on the practices of **assisted suicide, voluntary assisted dying** or **voluntary euthanasia**. These are the circumstances in which a person of sound mind, who has given consent, seeks to end their own life whether by their own hand, with the assistance of another, or by the hand of another.

In some quarters, suicide is now considered a pejorative term because of its association with such phenomena as "suicide bombers". In order to distance itself from these negative associations, Exit International, for example, employs the term, "rational suicide". This is defined as: "suicide by mentally competent individuals who are suffering from a serious medical illness or who reasonably envisage a future quality of life that they deem unacceptable."[16]

Dying with Dignity NSW states that it is now considered preferable to restrict use of the word 'suicide' to those persons taking their own life who would normally have gone on to live a happy and purposeful life with appropriate intervention.[17]

Groups lobbying for legalisation of assisted suicide contend that when a person voluntarily and freely wishes to terminate their own life, the law should either permit them to be provided with the means to do so, or authorise a doctor to do it for them. For the time being, however, any involvement with the suicide of another remains a criminal offence everywhere in Australia except, since 2019, in Victoria.

Although I have a religious faith (Christianity), I do not argue a Christian case against euthanasia and assisted suicide. My religious belief certainly informs my worldview; but a sound argument can be made against assisted dying without having to construct it upon a foundation of Christian ethics or anthropology.

My argument in this book is that when the state permits some of its citizens to be killed, a decisive blow is struck against the culture and tears the fabric both of civil society and of our common life. Legalising euthanasia will destroy family relationships, damage the trust we place in the medical profession, and corrode the bonds of civil society forged between individuals within communities.

Suicide in Australia: a national tragedy

Whether or not someone has a *right* to commit suicide, they certainly are *free* to do so. Exercising this freedom to end one's own life is coming to be seen as a mark of autonomy and independence of mind. But this view, although increasingly widely held, is mistaken because it ignores prevailing social proscriptions about suicide.

Suicide is a national tragedy and the leading cause of premature death in Australia – especially among people aged 15-24. According to figures from the Australian Bureau of Statistics (ABS), suicide is now the 15th leading cause of death in Australia, compared to the 14th leading cause in 2006.[18]

Use of age-standardised death rates allows the ABS to describe patterns of suicide in Australia. This makes it possible to draw comparison of death rates between different populations with different age structures.

In 2015, the overall suicide rate was 12.9 suicide deaths per 100,000 when 3,027 people died from intentional self-harm. This figure was up from 11.1 per 100,000 in 2013 (when 2,570 people committed suicide), and 10.5 per 100,000 in 2011 (when 2,393 people committed suicide). In 2020, the standardised death rate dropped slightly to 12.1 per 100,000 but the number of people who committed suicide rose to 3,139 – an average of about nine deaths per day.[19]

Men account for a little more than 75 per cent of deaths by suicide, but when it comes to overall rates of what the ABS calls "intentional self-harm deaths", younger age groups of both men and women comprise a higher proportion of those deaths with the highest rate (30.2 per cent) in the 20–24 age group.

Preliminary data show that in the group of males aged 40–44, 27.2 per 100,000 deaths were attributable to suicide, when 220 men killed themselves, compared with 70 female deaths by suicide (with an age-specific standardised death rate of 8.5 per 100,000) in the same age group.

According to the National Mental Health Commissioner, Ian Hickie, one of the factors accounting for the recent surge in suicide among middle-aged men is that men who were depressed during adolescence in the 1990s have carried suicidal ideation — that is, thinking seriously about suicide — into mid-life.[20]

For every death by suicide, it is estimated that as many as 30 people attempt to commit suicide – that is, there are an estimated 63,500 suicide attempts each year in Australia. Hospital data indicates that women are more likely to injure themselves than men. In the period 2008-2009, 62 per cent of those hospitalised due to self-harm were female.[21]

The contemporary weakening of the taboo against suicide will be considered later. A good place to begin, however, is by surveying the current laws in Australia concerning assisted suicide.

QUESTION 1

Where in Australia is assisted suicide legal?

Since this book was first published in 2018, the legal landscape regarding assisted suicide in Australia has changed considerably. Indeed, by late 2021, the only State not to have legalised euthanasia was New South Wales. Yet until only a few years ago, it was an offence everywhere in Australia, punishable by up to five years in prison, to incite, counsel or assist another to commit suicide or to attempt to commit suicide.

The historical reason why the law took this position is that suicide was long regarded as an offence against humankind. It was deemed to deprive one's family and community of a member prematurely and deny them the opportunity to care for the troubled individual. Criminal law codes, therefore, imposed sanctions for suicide and attempted suicide in the past because of their wider impact on society.

In many jurisdictions, the law has now changed. Suicide ceased to be a felony in England in 1961. Reform happened earlier than that in all Australian jurisdictions — much earlier in the case of New South Wales where the *Crimes Act 1900* (NSW) abolished the offence of suicide. Assisting suicide, however, was another matter.

The *Crimes Act 1900* (NSW) indicates clearly that one of the factors according to which an act causing death can amount to murder is where it has been done with the intent to kill another person. Accordingly, not only would a person counselling another to commit suicide commit a crime, the provision in any circumstances of the means to commit suicide, such as acceding to an individual's voluntary request for administration of a drug to bring about death, could well be construed as an act of murder.

In 2005, the Australian Parliament passed legislation making it illegal to produce, supply, or possess materials intended to promote the committing of suicide.[22] Even so, there have been few prosecutions for assisting another to commit suicide, and when a conviction has ensured, the decision of the court has often been based on the capacity of the deceased to give full consent.[23]

Most of the States have legalised voluntary assisted dying

The movement to decriminalise assisting another to commit suicide has gained considerable momentum in the last five years. Victoria was the first State to act when, in November 2017, the Parliament of Victoria passed the *Voluntary Assisted Dying Act 2017* (Victoria). The statute, which came into effect in mid-2019, allows an individual with a terminal illness to obtain a lethal drug within 10 days of asking to die after having completed a three-stage process involving two independent medical assessments. The law was based on recommendations of an expert panel chaired by a former president of the Australian Medical Association.

In order to qualify, an individual must be over the age of 18, have been resident in the State of Victoria for at least 12 months, and be suffering in a way that "cannot be relieved in a manner the person deems tolerable."[24] The law provides for self-administration of the lethal dose but permits a medical practitioner to administer the drugs if the patient is incapable of doing so for themselves. Subsequently, most States elsewhere in Australia adopted one form or another of this provision.

Since the voluntary assisted dying scheme began operating in Victoria, the Voluntary Assisted Dying Review Board has recorded a confirmed total of 331 deaths of people who have ingested medication.[25]

Euthanasia was next legalised in Western Australia when the State Parliament passed the *Voluntary Assisted Dying Act 2019* (WA) which came into effect in July 2021. The WA legislation followed that of Victoria closely with one important exception. In Victoria, it is not lawful for a medical practitioner to initiate a discussion about euthanasia. In Western Australia, however, a practitioner is permitted to initiate such a discussion on condition that the patient is informed of treatment and palliative care options *at the same time*.

A similar permission to initiate a discussion about euthanasia with a patient was subsequently adopted in Tasmania in 2021 in the *End-of-Life Choices (Voluntary Assisted Dying) Act 2021* (Tasmania). The law is due to come into effect in October 2022.

The Queensland Parliament also incorporated the Western Australian form of permission for a medical practitioner to initiate a discussion about euthanasia in the *Voluntary Assisted Dying Act 2021* (Queensland). This law will come into effect on 1 January 2023.

The Queensland law stirred particular controversy because it requires any health care or residential health care facility – including faith-based organisations that might have a moral or religious objection to euthanasia – to facilitate voluntary assisted dying for its residents. This is achieved by requiring a facility either to afford access by a medical practitioner so that a request for VAD can be made, or to transfer the patient to a place where such a request can be made.

When the Parliament of South Australia passed the *Voluntary Assisted Dying Act 2021* in June 2021, it chose not to permit medical practitioners to initiate any discussion about euthanasia with a patient. While the new law, which comes into effect in late 2022 or early 2023, does permit a facility to refuse to participate in voluntary assisted dying, it does impose similar obligations to those subsequently included in Queensland. It also grants the right not to participate in VAD in any way to health practitioners with conscientious objection to voluntary assisted dying.[26]

Until legislation comes into effect, voluntary assisted dying remains illegal in all States other than Victoria and Western Australia. All legislated VAD schemes provide for creation of an independent review board. The review board in Western Australia has yet to report at the time of writing (November 2021) because the legislation only came into effect in July 2021. The independent Voluntary Assisted Dying Review Board in Victoria issued its fifth report in August 2021.[27]

The last attempt to legalise euthanasia in New South Wales was launched in September 2017, a few weeks before the Victorian legislation received Royal Assent. The *Voluntary Assisted Dying Bill 2017*, introduced by Trevor Khan, MLC, had been drafted by a cross-party working group and contained provisions similar to those in Victoria's legislation. The bill was defeated by one vote in the State's Legislative Council.[28]

The Greenwich Bill

The *Voluntary Assisted Dying Bill 2021*, introduced by NSW MLA, Alex Greenwich, is an attempt to rectify the outcome of that vote and to bring NSW into line with the other States that have enacted euthanasia legislation.[29] But whereas the Khan Bill adopted the more conservative framework of what became the Victorian legislation, the Greenwich Bill adopts a number of measures similar to those included in Queensland, Western Australia, South Australia, and Tasmania.

Thus, for example, the Greenwich Bill permits a medical practitioner to raise the possibility of euthanasia so long as information about other treatment options and palliative care is provided at the same time (clause 10).

The Bill also proposes to follow Tasmania and Western Australia in permitting assessments of requests for voluntary assisted dying to be made by a medical practitioner via audio-visual communication such as telehealth (clause 182). Since the practitioner need not be the patient's treating physician, provision for audio-visual assessment means the Bill appears to make it possible for a doctor to approve VAD for a person they have never examined. Nor does the Bill require the "coordinating" or "consulting" practitioner to be a specialist in the patient's illness.

While there is provision in the Bill for referral if the coordinating practitioner is undecided (clauses 26 and 27), it is open to the practitioner to assess that the patient is likely to succumb to disease within 12 months without having had any history of treating the patient.

Part 5 of the Greenwich Bill also mirrors the South Australian and Queensland legislation in imposing requirements on faith-based organisations that might have a moral or religious objection to euthanasia. The Bill requires them to facilitate voluntary assisted dying for residents either by making information about VAD available to them, or by affording access by a medical practitioner so that a request for VAD can be made, or by arranging transfer of the patient to a place where such a request can be made.

In addition, the Greenwich Bill stipulates explicitly that death brought about by the ingestion of lethal medication in accordance with the voluntary assisted dying scheme does not constitute death by suicide (clause 12). This is in order to avoid conflict with life insurance policies that may impose restrictions when death occurs by suicide. A similar provision is contained in legislation passed in Western Australia, South Australia, and Queensland but not, apparently, in Tasmania or Victoria.

Within days of the Greenwich Bill being tabled in the NSW Legislative Assembly, it was referred to the Standing Committee of Law and Justice in the Legislative Council where it will be examined.[30] The Legislative Council committee will not report before the first sitting day of the new parliamentary session in February 2022 when it is likely the Bill will face the first in a series of amendments. At the time of writing (November 2021), procedural brakes have effectively been applied to the Bill's progress.

Voluntary assisted dying remains illegal in the Australian Capital Territory and the Northern Territory

Assisted suicide was legal between 1995 and 1997 in the Northern Territory after the legislature passed the *Rights of the Terminally Ill Act 1995* (NT) prepared by the Country Liberal government led by Marshall Perron.

The Commonwealth Parliament responded by passing a private member's bill promoted by Kevin Andrews, MP, which became the *Euthanasia Laws Act 1997*. The Act removed the power of any Australian territory to legalise euthanasia. The 1997 Act specifically repealed the Northern Territory Act – but not before Philip Nitschke had assisted three people to commit suicide.

Subsequently, in mid-2018, Senator David Leyonhjelm,[31] who professed a preoccupation with territory rights, once again proposed his own private member's bill – the *Restoring Territory Rights (Assisted Suicide Legislation) Bill 2015* – to restore the rights of the Northern Territory and the Australian Capital Territory to legislate on assisted suicide which had been set aside in 1997.

The Bill proposed by Senator Leyonhjelm simply recognised territory rights to legislate without specifying the scope of any legislation that might be passed in the Northern Territory or the Australian Capital Territory. The title of the bill made clear what kind of legislation he had in mind.

In the second reading speech delivered in the Senate on 3 March 2016, Leyonhjelm's principal concern was to assert the fundamental and legal right to make a choice about whether or not to continue living:

> The law says we are only permitted to die by our own hand, without assistance. And if we are too weak or incapacitated to end our lives ourselves, we are condemned to suffer until nature takes its course. It is a serious offence for anyone to either help us die, at our instruction, or even to tell us how to do it ourselves.[32]

The argument was cast, as so often, in terms of relief from a supposed experience of unendurable suffering. But the force of Leyonhjelm's reasoning meant that once permission to grant assistance is afforded to someone in pain, that permission must be extended *a fortiori* to anyone wishing to exercise their freedom to commit suicide. As Leyonhjelm remarked in his speech: "An individual may have good reasons to take his or her own life. But even if they do not, it is still their decision to make."[33]

If the principle of individual freedom entitles a sick person in pain to assistance in committing suicide, on what basis can that principle be denied to someone who is not sick and in pain – such as David Goodall – but who wishes to die?

Although the terminally ill are usually listed as the first and most obvious candidates for assisted suicide, the categories of eligibility are very elastic and can readily enough be extended to just about any person of any age who is tired of life. This is something admitted readily by former Liberal Senator Amanda Vanstone writing in support of Leyonhjelm's bill:

> There is no reason that we should refuse to end the suffering of two groups of people. First, those who have a terminal illness and are more worried about the quality of their remaining life than the quantity. Second, those for whom just age has taken its toll and whose consequent frailty leaves them incapable of doing much and who do not want to spend their last months being cared for as one does a baby.[34]

Senator Leyonhjelm's Bill was debated in the Senate in August 2018 but narrowly defeated by 36 votes to 34 votes after two days of debate. The defeat relieved the immediate pressure faced by the then Prime Minister, Malcolm Turnbull, to stop the Bill from reaching the House of Representatives. The Bill's defeat is unlikely to remove the topic of assisted dying from public debate, however.

Any future decision by the Commonwealth Parliament to enact a law legalising assisted suicide would also appear to conflict with government programs intended to prevent, or discourage, people from committing suicide. Legalisation of assisted suicide would, therefore, call into question the $85 million committed by the Turnbull Government in its 2018 Budget to fund suicide prevention programs.[35]

Successful passage of legislation in Victoria quickly encouraged euthanasia advocacy groups, such as Exit International and YourLastRight.com (a national alliance of dying-with-dignity and voluntary euthanasia societies in Australia), to increase pressure on politicians elsewhere to pursue reforms to legislation that have since swept across the country.

Whilst all opponents of assisted suicide are, at some time or another, bound to be cast as religious fanatics and bigots by their critics, it should be noted that not all calls for reform come from secular advocates. There are religious groups that favour assisted suicide. *Christians Supporting Choice for Euthanasia*, for example, claims that "the overwhelming majority of people of faith support choice for voluntary euthanasia", appealing to a 2007 survey conducted by Newspoll.[36]

Meanwhile, opposition to legalisation of assisted suicide in Australia comes from a broad cross-section of the community, some of whom are religious; others are not.

QUESTION 2
What does 'dying with dignity' mean?

Language is used in very elliptical ways in debate about euthanasia and assisted dying. One of the phrases that features prominently, and falls easily enough from the lips of many people in liberal democracies such as Australia, is "dying with dignity".

A coded phrase, it refers to the idea that each of us should be entitled to decide exactly how and when we die – as if an unexpected death, or one that comes as a result of illness rather than of our own volition, is by that very fact lacking in dignity. And, as in the case of David Goodall, one does not even need to be terminally ill to decide it is time to go.

"Dying with dignity" is almost promoted as little more than a lifestyle choice. "The state should no more intrude on personal decisions at the close of life than at any point during it," argued *The Economist*, mourning what it saw as an opportunity to reform the law on assisted suicide missed by the UK Parliament in September 2015. "Governments everywhere should recognise that, just as life belongs to the individual, so should its end."[37]

Respect for the dignity of the person is at the heart of arguments propounded by both advocates and opponents of assisted suicide.

The *Oxford English Dictionary* gives eight definitions for "dignity". The first two are the most relevant here: "the quality of being worthy or honourable; worthiness, worth, nobleness, excellence"; and "honourable or high estate, position or estimation; honour, degree of estimation, rank."[38]

Worthiness, excellence, and estimation, therefore, are the central notions of dignity which is a term of distinction and therefore not necessarily something to be found or expected in every human being. Dignity is clearly not synonymous with life because a person can live without dignity; but human life is obviously a necessary condition of there being human dignity, for without life there can be no possibility of dignity.

But what can it mean to "die with dignity"? In their appeals to dignity, those on either side of the debate about assisted suicide claim that their position is the ethically correct one. This seems paradoxical; but as Margaret Somerville, a bioethicist, has printed out, the paradox is resolved once we understand that each side uses the term human "dignity" differently.

According to Somerville, opponents of assisted suicide regard dignity as an *intrinsic* characteristic that human beings have simply by virtue of being human. It is a dignity that cannot be lost or diminished. A full conception of intrinsic human dignity is grounded in the inherent moral worth of human beings – a worth that is not diminished by disease or infirmity.

It should be noted, incidentally, that Somerville's interpretation does not completely accord with the *OED* definitions of dignity which indicate that dignity refers to worthiness and an honourable standing rather than to an inherent characteristic. It is quite possible to live without dignity. But Somerville's interpretation is helpful, nonetheless, in capturing a conception of the inherent value of human life.

In Somerville's view, pro-euthanasia advocates "see dignity as an extrinsic characteristic that can be lost with an individual's loss of autonomy, independence, and control." Providing assistance in suicide, pro-euthanasia advocates argue, is a means of restoring control and, thereby, safeguarding the dignity of the individual.[39]

This view of dignity aligns clearly more closely with the *OED* definition because it is a status that can be both gained and lost. And yet this extrinsic conception of human dignity is surely impoverished because it means that dignity, understood in this way, is always compromised by any form of disability or dependence.

But this cannot be correct: an individual can surely enjoy "the quality of being worthy or honourable" whilst living at the same time with disability or infirmity.

It is clear that the word, "dignity", is used in very different ways in the debate about assisted suicide, and that certain uses in various ways stretch the principally accepted meanings.

Some have argued, in response, that a subjective approach to dignity always needs to be adopted when discussing ways of dying: if a person *thinks* dying in a certain way lacks dignity, then it would undignified for that person to die in that way. "It is easy to see why this is popular," Christopher Coope, a moral philosopher writes, "for it seems to by-pass our problems with definitions, and it has an attractive air of autonomy about it."[40]

If the meaning of "death with dignity" were entirely subjective, however, its meaning would elude us. Dying without dignity would simply be a felt experience. It would commit us to holding that merely for a dying person to *think* they were dying without dignity would mean they actually *were* dying in such a manner.

There can be little doubt that fears about a loss of extrinsic — or *social* — dignity have been fueled, in part, by advances in medical technology that can allow people to live far longer than in earlier times.

In their arguments for people to be afforded relief from the ravages of technology, advocates of assisted suicide frequently appeal to compassion and emotion which can form a strong component of their case.

There are two elements to the argument from compassion The first element is that people who are terminally ill should not be forced to stay alive against their wishes and should be permitted to die when they choose.

This ignores the extremely important point that, if faced with medical intervention such as use of a respirator or a therapy such as kidney dialysis which is intended only to sustain life and alleviate pain rather than cure an illness, any person already has the right to refuse treatment, even if to do so may lead to an increased risk of death.

At first glance, assertion of a right to refuse treatment looks very like assertion of a "right to die". This is especially so since proponents of assisted suicide frequently demand not only discontinuation of treatment, but positive assistance in dying by, say, a lethal dose of a drug administered either by a physician or the individual patient.

But, as Somerville has argued, "A right to refuse treatment is based in a right to inviolability — a right not to be touched, including by treatment, without one's informed consent. It is not a right to die or a right to be killed."[41]

Although the call for discontinuation of treatment might look like assertion of a "right to die", it might also be described as assertion of a "right to commit suicide" or a "right to become dead". "At most, people have a negative content right to be allowed to die, not any right to positive assistance to achieve that outcome."[42] Perhaps it is more accurate to say a person is *free* to become dead.

Proponents of assisted suicide often insist that because the outcome is the same, there is no significant difference between deliberately withdrawing essential medical life support and deliberate intervention to bring about death. But there is a most significant difference.

Letting a patient die at some point is a practical condition of the successful operation of modern medicine, as Yale Kamisar[43] has observed. The same cannot be said of physician-assisted suicide:

> To allow a patient to reject unwanted bodily intrusions by a physician is hardly the same thing as granting her a right to determine the time and manner of her death. The distinction between a right to resist invasive medical procedures and the right to [physician-assisted suicide] is a comprehensible one and a line maintained by almost all major Anglo-American medical associations.[44]

The second limb of the argument from compassion seeks to spare vulnerable patients who are experiencing what is usually described "unbearable pain". Yet available data suggest the experience of unbearable pain is not a principal reason why people request assisted suicide.

In Oregon, USA, data summaries under the *Death with Dignity Act 1997* (DWDA) record details of those who have taken advantage of the Oregon law's permission to end one's life by means of a voluntarily self-administered lethal dose of medications. The summaries are thua a reasonably reliable guide to what motivates people to seek a lethal dose. A total of 1905 people have died from ingesting lethal medication since the law was passed in 1997.

According to the DWDA Data Summary for 2020, published in February 2021, 370 people in Oregon received prescriptions for lethal medication in 2020. As of January 2021, 245 people were reported to have died in 2020 from ingesting the medication.

Of these, 80 people (33 per cent) gave inadequate pain control as their reason for seeking assisted suicide; for 92 people (38 per cent), it was loss of control of bodily functions; for 130 people (53 per cent), it was concern about becoming a burden on others; for 176 people (72 per cent), the reason was loss of dignity; and for 231 people (94 per cent), it was a loss of the ability to engage in activities making life enjoyable.[45]

Unlike the Oregon DWDA data summaries, reports from Victoria's Voluntary Assisted Dying Review Board, which represent the only data sets available to date in Australia, provide no information about the reasons given by patients for availing themselves of voluntary assisted dying.

If the Oregon DWDA report figures are typical of other places where assisted suicide is available, however, it would appear that relief from intolerable pain is the reason for seeking assistance in only a minority of cases. Anxiety about loss of ability to participate in society and loss of autonomy are by far the more prevalent reasons.

The fact that few people appear to seek a lethal dose because of intolerable pain distinctly undermines arguments based on compassion that are advanced by proponents. Critics such as Kevin Yuill[46] are quite skeptical about the argument from compassion: "Much of what passes for compassion is simply reflected fear on the part of those with little prospect of death in the immediate future. [It] is really self-centred fear for one's own prospects."[47]

Flaws in the argument from compassion arise, in part, because of its close association with the questionable concept of "dignity" to which proponents of assisted suicide appeal. Notwithstanding the problems identified earlier with her own analysis of dignity, Somerville's account is certainly helpful because it lays bare the subjective element of responses individuals make to the prospect of death.

Thus, when people advocating legalisation of assisted suicide appeal to "dignity", the dignity to which they refer, and which it is held to be important to retain, does appear to be the *social* dignity of independence and capacity and not the intrinsic *human* dignity that comes simply from the fact of human *being*.

This still offers little help in understanding what the phrase, "dying with dignity", actually means. Death happens to everyone: as Shakespeare tells us, "Death, a necessary end, will come when it will come."[48]

While it is true that one can die in undignified circumstances — by car crash, execution, or torture, for example – such a death can, at the same time, surely be dignified if the person confronting death does so with a certain spirit of worthiness, nobleness, and honour.

The dignity with which death is met is not determined by external circumstances. Indeed, it is difficult to understand how the sort of death that occurs naturally can be either dignified or undignified, as observed by Leon Kass, a physician and philosopher:

> A death with dignity — which may turn out to be something rare or uncommon even under the best circumstances — entails more than the absence of external indignities. Dignity in the face of death cannot be given or conferred from the outside but requires a dignity of soul in the human being who faces it.[49]

Dignity in the face of death is a possibility for everyone as they die; it is something that depends on the character and bearing of the individual who is dying.

Thus, if the meaning of "death with dignity" is entirely subjective, dying without dignity will simply be a felt experience. It will mean that merely for a dying person to *think* they were dying without dignity would mean they actually *were* dying in such a manner.

Concern for addressing the "felt" experience of lost social dignity by the patient lies behind emergence of a form of psychotherapeutic intervention known as "dignity therapy" pioneered by Harvey Max Chochinov, a psychiatrist.[50]

Dignity therapy seeks to mitigate a loss of social dignity and help patients to understand that ingesting a lethal dose of medication is not the best way to restore that dignity. For opponents of euthanasia, such as Somerville, dignity therapy offers their case significant weight:

> [Dignity therapy] identifies the reasons people want

> euthanasia, explains why many of them change their minds, and describes in personal detail what they and others would have lost if [physician-assisted suicide and euthanasia] were available. Dignity therapy can assist health-care professionals to help patients at the end of their lives who see their circumstances as unbearable and have lost a "why" to re-find one.[51]

The notion of "dying with dignity" advocated by proponents of euthanasia and physician-assisted suicide reflects a state of *pre-mortem* anxiety and loneliness that can beset the terminally ill; a lethal injection which cuts life short is hardly an appropriate way to address this experience of distress or despair. Dignity therapy, increasingly available as a component of palliative care in Australia, enables the terminally ill to reclaim their identity and sense of social dignity.

The phrase, "dying with dignity", as deployed by proponents of legalising assisted suicide is thereby exposed as meaning precious little. It is used for rhetorical effect to describe the state that precedes death and not the death itself.

Once the categories of eligibility for assisted suicide and voluntary euthanasia extend beyond terminal illness and the experience of "unbearable suffering" — as they already have done in the case of David Goodall — the dignity ascribed to the *pre-mortem* state will, soon enough, turn upon vulnerability, weakness, and infirmity.

Question 2

In the 20th century, we witnessed the consequences of the profound contempt shown, at times, for the weak and the infirm. Now it is important to affirm that those human conditions do not rob — and must never be allowed to rob — any person of the dignity they possess.

QUESTION 3

Does personal autonomy justify legalising assisted suicide?

Anxiety about loss of social dignity is frequently expressed in terms of the conviction that individual freedom means a person is always entitled to decide for herself what makes life good, and how she will conduct her life in pursuit of that good.

Individual freedom is closely linked to the notion of personal autonomy, something that lies at the heart of the argument for legalising assisted suicide.

"Autonomy" is defined by the *Oxford English Dictionary* as "the liberty to follow one's will; control over one's own affairs; freedom from external influence, personal independence."[52] "Autonomy", therefore, entails the twin notions of *liberty* and *agency*.

First, appeal is made to autonomy in support of the idea that an individual who wishes to die ought to be freed from any external restriction or restraint, and be able to follow her will. Second, the appeal to autonomy seeks support for the claim that she ought to be afforded the full capacity to act intentionally to bring about the desired outcome of her own death.

Freedom from constraint and the granting of capacity are held to extend to deciding the timing of, the manner of, and the control over one's death. Anything less, it is argued, compromises the autonomy of the individual.

If an individual really does seek to act with autonomy, however, why is such effort directed to harnessing the authority of the state to enable the exercise of autonomy? Advocates for legalisation of assisted suicide are actually creating a dependence on the state for doing the very thing that an individual is already free to do – that is, to commit suicide.

Perhaps what advocates really seek is not a commitment by the state to the principle of autonomy, but approval in advance of individual acts of suicide. "There is a big leap between freedom to take one's life and the freedom to 'obtain assistance' or be euthanized," according to Kevin Yuill, a critic of legalising assisted suicide.[53] Advocates of legalisation, ironically, undermine, rather than uphold, individual autonomy:

> Whereas much of the assisted suicide lobby sees itself as liberatory, ridding citizens of pointless laws based on outmoded moral systems that prevent individuals from doing what they wish, they in reality call for government assistance and further regulation of a sphere formerly administered privately.[54]

The concept of autonomy is more contentious for advocates of assisted suicide than many of them care to admit. There are two principal difficulties.

The first difficulty is that, used in a purely descriptive way, autonomy does little more than identify the conditions necessary for identifying an action as self-governed, such as freedom of choice, or freedom to act. Since both a vicious and a virtuous act can be performed autonomously, the concept of autonomy is of little use when it comes to justifying an action.

The second difficulty is that if autonomy is used to *justify* a particular act and thereby ascribe a moral quality to that act, something more needs to be said about the broader moral context of the act in order to distinguish the virtuous act from the vicious one.

When actions performed autonomously are criminalised by society – such as stealing the property of another – it is clear that the autonomy of, in this case, a thief is impeded. Actions cannot be sanctioned as morally good simply because they are performed autonomously: there must be something more. As John Safranek[55] has remarked:

> Autonomy is necessary for the existence of a moral act but is insufficient to justify one. The justification of the act will hinge on the end to which autonomy is employed. It is not autonomy per se that vindicates an autonomy claim but the good that autonomy is instrumental in achieving.[56]

This is a critical point when it comes to an action such as assisted suicide. Autonomy, alone, cannot be invoked to justify the act; appeal must also be made to an underlying moral conception of what is good, and which the act strives to attain. But what is that underlying moral good?

Conflicting conceptions of the good feature in debate about legalisation of assisted suicide. This conflict embraces differing conceptions of dignity and differing conceptions of the inherent value of human life. It is this conflict about conceptions of the good that really lies at the heart of debate about assisted suicide. It is not a dispute about autonomy, dignity, or the right to die.

A further important point, frequently overlooked, is that an appeal to autonomy in support of legalising assisted suicide is inconsistent with the restrictions placed on its availability.

Eligibility is strictly constrained in those States of Australia where voluntary assisted dying schemes have been legalised. For example, a person must be suffering from an incurable disease expected to cause death within six months (or 12 months in the case of a neuro-degenerative condition) in order to be eligible to seek physcian-assisted suicide. In Queensland, the specified time frame for all conditions is 12 months.

Such a constraint serves only to restrict real freedom rather than support it. If individual autonomy really is a ground for obtaining assistance in dying, all requests from competent individuals ought to be honoured regardless of life expectancy.

Furthermore, people diagnosed with a mental illness are also specifically excluded from assisted suicide schemes in Australia; but it is, surely, inconsistent to restrict the availability of assisted suicide to those enduring physical suffering and exclude those enduring psychological suffering.

Appeals to autonomy must entail approving *all* suicides. No justification could exist for approving one request for assistance with dying, of which advocates approved, but denying another of which they did not.

If the autonomy argument for legalising assisted suicide were to prevail, appeal could be made neither to compassion as a ground for granting assistance, nor to mercy. This inconsistency seriously undermines arguments for assisted suicide based on appeals to autonomy.

QUESTION 4

Why do claims to a 'right to die' threaten the common good?

Proponents of assisted suicide claim ownership of the end of life. They argue that in doing so they are upholding a key principle of individual freedom. Freedom is a basic good, they say, and any prohibition of assisted suicide is an unwarranted restriction on an individual's freedom to choose how — and for how long — they wish to live.

Appealing to individual autonomy, proponents argue that nothing, including the moral beliefs of others, should ever constrain the individual's freedom to commit suicide. In appealing to autonomy, these advocates seek to convert individual freedom into a "right to die".

Yet this absolutist view of autonomy amounts to asserting that the desire or the choice — or even the need — to die must be understood as a *right* to die. Choice is paramount; but choice has little to do with "rights".

Declaring the freedom to do something is very different from declaring that individuals have a *right* to do it. Neither a need nor a desire is identical to a right. Each of us is free to choose to do all kinds of things: to commit burglary; to murder; and to drive under the influence of alcohol. The law does not stop us from committing any such acts; it simply stipulates the consequences we will have to bear if we do commit them — and get caught.

But when a particular outcome is desired, rights-based language is frequently deployed in an attempt to turn a freedom to choose that outcome into a right that supposedly guarantees an entitlement to the outcome. As Penney Lewis, Co-Director of the Centre of Medical Law & Ethics at King's College, London, has observed, "Transforming an argument into the form of a right increases its palatability and persuasive force."[57]

Advocates of the "right to die" are using the language of rights in their crusade to win moral and legal acceptance not only for the idea that human life is not inviolable but also for the primacy of rights over other forms of moral discourse.

Rights language has such popular and political force, in Lewis's view, that it often obscures those other forms, particularly arguments about duties — that is, those specific obligations, legal or moral, that are owed to others and flow from one's participation in civil society:

> Arguments which are not in the form of rights, such as those premised on duties, do not truly disappear from the debate, but rather are transformed into rights discourse while their original form remains covert and unrecognized.[58]

The eclipse of duties that are "other-concerning" by rights that are "self-concerning" is critically important. When calls for freedom to be allowed to become dead are couched in the language of rights, they tend to conceptualise a society composed mainly of self-interested individuals intent upon severing all social ties and obligations when they see fit. In such a society, no one owes anything to anyone. This is why assertion of the right to die is what the philosopher, Sir Roger Scruton, describes as a "claim right" in contrast to a "freedom right".[59]

According to Scruton, "freedom rights", such as the right to free movement and the right to property, allow an individual to establish a sphere of personal sovereignty from which that person can negotiate behaviour in relation to others.

A freedom right amounts to a justified demand made against others that they refrain from interfering with the individual. It is observed or respected by non-invasion or non-action thereby enabling us to establish a society in which consensual relations are the norm. Freedom rights do this by defining for each individual the sphere of sovereignty from which others are excluded.

Claim rights, by contrast, are asserted as a *claim* upon a non-specific benefit such as education, health, a standard of living, or even compensation. They are simply demands that someone else do something or give something that the one demanding has an interest in their doing or giving.

Scruton argues that assertion of the "right to die" is the assertion of a "claim right" because, while it is thought to allow the individual to express sovereignty over her or his life, it simply presumes an obligation owed by the state to the individual — but one that is neither negotiated nor reciprocal.

In asserting this claim right, the individual, alone, decides whether or not life is worth living; her or his decision is not to be overridden by any other institution or structure, whether the state, the church, or the family.

This conviction that autonomous individuals are quite free to define their own conceptions of the good, regardless of the concerns of others, is supposedly warranted by the presumption of human dignity. This, in turn, is intimately connected with self-respect and the paramount status of individual choice: if this is what I want, I am justified in demanding it in virtue of my autonomous status as a human being. But as Leon Kass[60] has remarked, this assertion of autonomy marks a troubling development:

> In civil society, the natural rights of self-preservation, secured through active but moderate self-assertion, have given way to the non-natural rights of self-creation and self-expression; the new rights have no connection to nature or reason, but appear as the rights of the untrammelled will.[61]

The notion of the inherent worth of the individual lies at the very heart of the concept of human rights. Human beings are due a certain minimal respect — which includes the inviolability of human life — simply in virtue of their being human. This is the very inviolability that guarantees abuses such as torture are always objectively and absolutely wrong.

Once discussion of rights is given precision by making the distinction between claim rights and freedom rights, the matter at the heart of the argument for legalising assisted suicide becomes clear. It is nothing less than a call for acceptance and normalisation of adult killing by consent. It sanctions a conception of individual autonomy whereby a person's self-determination can only be effected by the physical (and moral) assistance of another person.

With that development, assisted suicide is no longer solely a matter of self-determination. It becomes what Daniel Callahan[62] has described as "a mutual, social decision between two people, the one to be killed and other to do the killing."[63]

This represents a move, in other words, from *my* right to self-determination to the *doctor's* right to kill me once I have given the doctor permission to take my life. But what warrant can there be for such a move? Callahan calls into question the idea that the autonomy of the self-directing individual must always take precedence over the wider good of the community:

> The idea that we can waive our right to life, and then give to another the power to take that life, requires a justification yet to be provided by anyone. Consenting adult killing, like consenting adult slavery or degradation, is a strange route to human dignity.[64]

Advocates of assisted suicide emphasise the rights and autonomy of the individual seeking to end her life. But more attention needs to be paid to the moral position of the doctor who does the killing.

Whatever the grounds on which a person seeks medical assistance, each involves, in one way or another, a claim about subjective experience. It might be the burden of intolerable suffering, a fear of disability or the decreasing ability to participate in society, or a feeling that dignity has been lost. But these judgments are all subjective.

Faced with similar circumstances of impaired health, some people will always find life more of a benefit than a burden; others will find pain more bearable, even if uncomfortable. Suffering is surely as much a function of the world view, and also the temperament and disposition, of the individual concerned as it is of the condition with which they are afflicted.

In agreeing to administer a lethal dose, a doctor would be responding as much to the world view and values of the patient as to the medical condition itself. Without an objective way of assessing the claims of the patient, on what basis is a doctor to weigh the claim that life is no longer worth living?

Whatever merit there is to the idea of a right to die – and the argument here is that it bears little merit – it is clear that assisted suicide is never a purely private matter of the self-determination of the individual. As Callahan emphasises, "It is an act that requires two people to make it possible, and a complicit society to make it acceptable."[65]

Liberal societies have long sought to limit the circumstances in which one person can take the life of another and have based the limits on a fundamental respect for human life.

These limits included restrictions on ownership of guns; restrictions on consumption of alcohol, and now drugs, when driving; restrictions on use of physical force; and abolition of capital punishment. Yet, at the same time as these legal constraints are broadly welcomed and accepted, advocates of assisted suicide are seeking to waive the principle of the inviolability of human life and to sanction a new category of killing in which the medical profession is specifically and actively involved.

The principle of individual autonomy is not a moral absolute. By attempting to waive our personal inviolability, we will perpetrate a greater harm both on those around us, and on society as a whole; for, as Neil Scolding, a neuroscientist, has warned, "the impact of our choices and actions on society has always overridden autonomy in such instances."[66]

The common good of the community and the health of society is bound to be harmed if the new category of killing by means of assisted suicide wins acceptance.

While an individual can certainly *choose* to end her life and may *desire* to do so, the idea that there exists a *right* to do so is not merely erroneous. By harming the web of social relations and obligations comprising family and community life, the claim to a "right to die" actually threatens to tear at the fabric of civil society and do irreparable harm to the social roles and attachments constitutive of individual identity.

QUESTION 5

Why should the state prevent me from ending my own life?

Every death by intentional self-harm has a profound impact on others. It is often the case that such a death causes great emotional trauma among the family, friends, and community of the deceased.

Grief is likely to be compounded by complicated feelings of guilt – and even anger – about what the deceased has done, particularly so when the suicide is an aggressive act directed at others.

Suicide is a specifically human action of self-destruction, defined by the *Oxford English Dictionary* as "the act of taking one's life; self-murder."[67] In virtue of the intentionality behind the act, a person intent upon suicide, therefore, has a moral responsibility both for the decision and for the committing of the act.

Laws against suicide in many Western countries – including Australia — were reformed extensively in the 20th century, and it is no longer a crime to kill oneself, or to attempt to do so, except in Cyprus.[68]

Suicide does remain illegal in some countries in Africa and South-East Asia, however. Someone who succeeds in killing themselves is, obviously enough, beyond the reach of the law. But legal sanctions can extend to disposal of the suicide's estate, disposal of the corpse, and the rights of family members.

In Western, liberal democracies, reform of the law against suicide reflects a step to remove the involvement of the state in issues which are largely regarded as moral. Abolition of the criminal offence of committing suicide does not confer a legal *right* to do so, nor does it signify the state's approval of suicide.

Nonetheless, *freedom* to commit suicide is properly considered both pre-political and pre-legal. Whatever the law says, killing oneself is always a possibility, something that any competent human being can achieve irrespective of what the law states.

Notwithstanding removal of legal penalties for committing – or attempting to commit – suicide, there remains a social taboo surrounding suicide in countries including Australia: "The essentially private gesture of ending one's own life has long been met with public indignation and dealt with as an act of criminality or lunacy."[69]

A taboo is a social custom offering protection from that which society deems an inherently harmful practice. The words and phrases used to convey the apparent reasonableness of normalising assisted suicide — "dying with dignity", "euthanasia", and "deliverance" — are all euphemisms intended to break that taboo.

Those phrases serve to weaken the taboo surrounding

suicide by placing some distance between the comforting notion of a decision freely taken and the stark fact that they actually describe deliberate termination of human life by one's own hand or with the assistance of another.

The roots of the taboo surrounding suicide lie deep within Christianity. Christianity makes an important distinction between the willing surrender of one's life (for example, as a sacrificial act in defence of another) and the deliberate taking of one's life.

It was not always thus. In the ancient world, suicide was widely considered to be justified if life became unbearable, and was considered an honourable course of action for a virtuous person – usually a man – faced with intolerable circumstances. If life were to become bitter, suicide was an obvious and acceptable solution. As Marcus Aurelius observed in *Meditations*:

> Depart at once from life, not in passion, but with simplicity and freedom and modesty, after doing this one laudable thing at least in this life, to have gone out of it thus.[70]

Choice was paramount, and an individual was considered to be free to end the travails of life whenever he (most usually) or she chose to do so.

Social attitudes to suicide began to change with the coming of Christianity — particularly with the influence of Saint Augustine in the 5th century — which teaches that a human being is not the author of a life nor its absolute owner.

According to Christian doctrine, life is a gift entrusted by God that it may find its fulfilment in the loving service of God and of other human beings. It is not for the individual to decide for how long that gift shall be so used. To end one's own life by a deliberate and premediated act, therefore, was to make a strike both against God and against the community. Suicide was held to be an outright denial of the divine will, and a heinous sin because repentance was impossible.

The theological effect of Christian teaching on wider social views concerning suicide has abated somewhat while increasing attention has been paid to the psychopathology of suicide. Indeed, the importance of support ministries for the suicidal is shown by the extensive use made of such ministries since The Samaritans was established in London in 1953.

The criminal law presents no solution to the crises and difficulties that are likely to prompt an individual to take their own life. But there is a much broader acceptance that the decision to commit suicide is a symptom of a deeper mental or spiritual disturbance.

Hence, the societal taboo surrounding suicide remains in place and is evidenced by the embarrassment experienced by many people when they are confronted with, or have to talk about, acts of suicide. Even if the language used has evolved, there is still something of the stigma around suicide identified in an important, if overlooked, essay by Sidney Hook[71] in 1927:

> Suicide has been interpreted as indicating a dry-rot of the soul, as a perverse and pernicious setting-at-nought of all human values, and finally as a cowardly flight from the duties and burdens to which human flesh is heir.[72]

In his analysis of the morality of suicide, Hook argues that suicide is permissible in certain circumstances, but that society needs to inculcate programs of moral teaching in order to make even permissible suicides rare. He has little time for many of the traditional arguments against suicide (drawn largely from Christian notions about duty owed to God). Nor does Hook consider suicide intrinsically cowardly or a violation of human dignity.

The argument against suicide that Hook does find forceful is the harm it inflicts upon one's friends and family. Although not an absolute argument – "for it does not touch that individual whose spiritual roots are not strongly intertwined with those of his [sic] fellows"[73] – the argument against harming friends recognises that suicide is a social act, a point emphasised by Robert Talisse, a philosopher, in some retrospective comments about Hook's argument:

> The argument properly locates the question of the morality of suicide within the complex matrix of socially mediated moral relations. What makes a given act of suicide wrong is not that it breaches obligations to ourselves, God, or the state, but rather that it violates associative duties to particular others.[74]

Locating suicide within a social network of relations and connections is important for understanding why the taboo of suicide persists, even though the impact on society of Christian teaching about it has diminished. While the decision to commit suicide is both personal and private, once acted upon, the decision becomes entirely social.

It may be taboo to commit suicide, but it is not illegal; an individual is *free* to commit suicide, but there is no *right* in law to do so. And while there is a freedom to commit suicide, it is merely a freedom to breach the norms prevailing within an existing moral structure. It does not extend to being a freedom to have the act of suicide exonerated.[75]

But suicide remains an action taken *within* that moral structure. The limits are breached, not altered. As such, this means that the moral perspectives shared by members of society will always be brought to bear in appraising an act of suicide as either a good act or a bad one. For Yuill, this goes to the heart of the argument about why it is important to resist the legalisation of assisted suicide:

> In attempting to redefine self-destruction in neutral terms – as medical treatment rather than a dramatic act – it robs us of our ability to come to some collective decision on the rightness or wrongness of the suicide.[76]

This explains why the rhetoric of rights, used to promote the idea of a dignified and even noble death, entails a grotesque inversion of the very principle of a "right".

Developed for the protection and preservation of the individual against the demands both of the state and other individuals, the language of rights has now been commandeered to promote the wants and demands of the "self" that include the desire for self-negation.

For thinkers such as Leon Kass, the rights rhetoric has little to do with the protective function of human rights but is concerned solely with trying to fathom some of the immensely complex moral problems that confront the individuated "self":

> In trying to batter our way through the human condition with the bludgeon of personal rights, we allow ourselves to be deceived about the most fundamental matters, about our unavoidable finitude, and about the sustaining interdependence of our lives. [77]

Perhaps the assertion of the right to die is, after all, best understood as a complaint, borne of human pride, against the injustice meted out by nature against human beings ill-fated, as we all are, to die. "The ill-fated demand a right not to be ill-fated," says Kass. "Those who want to die, but cannot, claim a right to die."[78]

The inevitability of death may be an affront to human pride, and the desire not to be thus ill-fated held privately, and with conviction. But the act of suicide can never be regarded as either neutral or completely private.

Legalising assisted suicide, therefore, poses threats to the social and cultural fabric that far outweigh any consideration about whether or not a particular act of suicide can be justified.

QUESTION 6

Why are fears about descending the 'slippery slope' justified?

One warning, central to debate about legalising assisted suicide and euthanasia, has been expressed as the "slippery slope" argument. This is the argument that an action which itself seems unobjectionable would set in motion a series of events that would lead to an undesirable and, indeed, unintended outcome.

Opponents of legalisation have argued that if the practice of mercy killing were introduced, it would not long be confined to voluntary euthanasia. Soon enough, the argument goes, pressure would be brought to bear on the vulnerable and incompetent to end their lives, and they would be killed without their consent. And down the slippery slope our society would slide.

The slippery slope argument about euthanasia can be expressed more precisely in this way: once one accepts X (voluntary euthanasia for the terminally ill) on the basis of principle P (for example, personal autonomy), one is bound to accept Y (voluntary euthanasia for those who are not terminally, or even physically, ill). If Y is considered abhorrent, then P must be flawed, and therefore X must be rejected.

Thus, adopting a practice at the top of the slope (proposition *X*) can lead to adoption of an objectionable practice (proposition *Y*) at the bottom of the slope. The idea is that between the top and the bottom there are many little steps, and the slope is slippery because it is so difficult to know where to draw the line.

Philosophers are often critical of the slippery slope argument because, for example, the more steps there are on the slope, the less secure is the route from *X* to *Y*. This can lead to instances of exaggerated rhetoric and inflated claims about possible — but probably unlikely — outcomes.

A topical example of such slippery slope rhetoric is the overblown argument that if the Commonwealth Parliament were to legislate to protect religious freedom, this will inevitably lead down the slope to introduction of *sharia* law in Australia, widely considered to be an undesirable outcome.

On the other hand, a seemingly insignificant change, such as restricting sale of cigarettes by removing vending machines, can lead (and has, in fact, led) to a major change in social practice — a total ban on all smoking in all public places and spaces.

Changes of practice in areas such as public health are often sought by means of a series of small steps. Efforts to change social attitudes to alcohol, for example, are led by policy steps such as increases in taxation followed by public information campaigns, which are then followed, in turn, by legislated restrictions on marketing, sales, and consumption.

When what might be called a stepped, or incremental, approach to public policy change is adopted, it is appropriate to think about where the first of those steps might lead.

There are times when a concern about what things will be like at the bottom of the slope justifies great caution about a decision made at the top. Charles Camosy, an ethicist, has expressed particular concern about problems inherent in adopting the practice of euthanasia as a public policy:

> Human beings are prone to push boundaries and hijack accepted practices for self-serving and even destructive purposes. There is no reason to think that euthanasia would be an exception to this rule – especially given the dominance of consumerism and hyper-autonomy in our current social climate.[79]

Thus, a principal concern about legislating for assisted suicide is that the categories of people eligible to request it will continually expand.

Most proponents of assisted suicide in Australia discuss the matter in terms of the rights or needs of the terminally ill – that is, of those people with a medical condition which causes unbearable suffering and is highly likely to produce death in six to twelve months.

There are others, however, who are not terminally ill but who, nonetheless, find life imposes upon them a burden of "unbearable suffering".

It seems arbitrary to exclude a person suffering from an incurable and progressive disease; or a person who has a severe physical disability; or someone with severe mental illness; or a person severely disfigured owing to an accident.

It is also contended, for example, that pressure to die will mount on those who feel they are a burden on their families or on health care systems. Why should availability of assisted suicide be confined only to those with a terminal illness?

As societal views about killing change, it will be considered reasonable to grant permission to anyone who declares that life, for them, has become intolerable. And, soon enough, it is feared, assisted suicide will slide into voluntary euthanasia, and then into involuntary euthanasia – all the consequence of more casual attitudes to killing.

Assisted suicide and voluntary euthanasia are now legal practices in some jurisdictions. Therefore, a good way to test the cogency of slippery slope arguments is to look at evidence from those jurisdictions to see whether it bears out existence of a slippery slope.

Perhaps that evidence even bears out the ambitious claim that the practice of assisted suicide can be regulated effectively without adversely affecting the vulnerable or making attitudes to killing more casual.

Evaluating available evidence is not quite as straightforward as it might seem. The difficulty in drawing international comparisons is compounded by the challenge of discovering just how much practice falls outside regulations and reporting. As there is little consensus as to interpretation of available data, advocates and opponents draw from it the conclusions they wish to see.[80]

Put thus, arguments about descending a slippery slope can seem pointless. The question at the heart of the matter is whether or not intentional killing of individuals by themselves (or by doctors) can be permitted without the danger of sliding to a position where society's general commitment to the intrinsic value of human life is diminished.

One thinker who argues that there is a well-founded anxiety about the possibility of containing the deliberate killing of patients – or the cooperation of doctors – once the practice of assisted suicide is established is Nigel Biggar, a moral theologian.

Biggar has closely analysed competing – and complex – evaluations of evidence from the Netherlands where the practice of voluntary euthanasia became legally acceptable in 1984 following a decision of the Supreme Court of the Netherlands. He examined evidence that, since 1984, attitudes to death may have changed and the categories of eligibility may have become more elastic. In doing so, he relied on the very comprehensive study of the situation in the Netherlands carried out by John Keown.[81]

Keown's study was extremely detailed, as was Biggar's analysis of the study.[82] It is therefore not practicable here to do more than sketch in outline Biggar's evaluation of Keown's conclusions; nor than simply to summarise the conclusions that Biggar, himself, drew in the course of his own analysis.

In outline, Keown found, first, that the guidelines for the practice of voluntary euthanasia are too imprecise and that the key concept of "unbearable suffering" is too elastic. Second, Keown concluded that the checks imposed on the medical profession were not sufficiently rigorous.

When he proceeded to analyse surveys of the practice of euthanasia in the Netherlands, Keown found evidence to suggest that, within six years of the promulgation of guidelines for voluntary euthanasia, the practice of *non-*voluntary euthanasia had become more frequent.

Yet critics of Keown, such as John Griffiths, argue that his study failed to establish, first, that the practice of voluntary euthanasia increased and evolved into non-voluntary euthanasia after it became legal; and, second, that there is a causal relationship between legalisation and the emergence of non-voluntary euthanasia.[83]

On the basis of his analysis of Keown's study and the critique of Griffiths, Biggar drew a sobering conclusion about the slipperiness of the slope facing a society that legislates to permit assisted suicide:

> It is surely reasonable to suppose that the modification of the law to permit hitherto forbidden killing on the very elastic condition [of unbearable suffering] is bound to have encouraged the taking of patients' lives in a much wider range of circumstances than before.[84]

Has evolution of this practice led to a moral degeneration in Dutch society? This is an extremely difficult question to answer with precision – something Biggar readily conceded.

Nonetheless, he is concerned that in the absence of the tightest restrictions on the circumstances in which a person may be killed, the categories of eligibility – in particular, the elasticity of "unbearable suffering" – will expand, leading to a moral slide. Indeed, Biggar is so concerned about the consequences of slipping down the slope that he affirmed the priority of helping those in pain to flourish as much as the limits of their suffering permit:

> This is stronger than the obligation to relieve human beings of suffering that permanently precludes any such flourishing. To permit such relief by voluntary euthanasia or assisted suicide would be to jeopardise society's human ethos.[85]

His conclusion rests on Keown's empirical research which was confined to the Netherlands. Other jurisdictions do not necessarily fit the Dutch pattern.

Oregon, for example, legalised assisted suicide in 1997 and maintains detailed data summaries of those who have availed themselves of lethal doses of medication. Successive annual Oregon Death with Dignity Act (DWDA) Data Summaries indicate a steady rise in the number of deaths each year.

In 1998, 16 people died by ingesting medication; five years later, in 2002, 38 people died. The number of DWDA deaths rose to 49 in 2007; this figure rose to 85 deaths in 2012. In 2017, the number of recorded DWDA deaths was

143; and in 2020, the number had risen to 245 deaths. The total number of DWDA deaths for the period, 1998-2020, was 2,895.[86]

Although the general trend of DWDA deaths in the period, 1997-2020, is upwards, the rise hardly represents a sharp spike in deaths; and each year the number of DWDA deaths is lower than the number of those who received DWDA prescriptions for medication (also recorded), but did not ingest the lethal dose. There is no reliable evidence that patients are being put to death without their consent.

Many more generations of data are needed before anything approaching a final determination is possible. If Keown's findings are found generally acceptable, it is clearly the case that slippage is possible and, perhaps, in time, inevitable.

And if the principle of individual autonomy is given precedence above all else and made the touchstone for assisted suicide, it is difficult to see how, in time, the preferences of the individual *could* be contained by regulation, no matter how rigorous.

Legalising assisted suicide would entail inviting doctors, and even the courts, to weigh the reasons a person has for wanting to end their life. Such an invitation could come to be considered an intolerable intrusion upon the privacy and autonomy of the individual patient as objective criteria are brought to bear on what is a very intimate and personal decision.

This could be especially so in a society where a perceived pressure on medical resources, combined with a cultural environment in which older people are made to feel an unwelcome burden, leads to opportunities for the elderly to end their lives more easily. As Camosy has remarked:

> Ironically, it is a hyper-focus on autonomy which is *facilitating* a slide down precisely the kind of slippery slope such a focus was supposed to avoid. It turns out that in a consumerist, youth-worshipping culture, giving older persons the choice to kill themselves makes them anything but free. [Italics in original][87]

Regulation will not be able to contain the concept of "unbearable suffering". It will have to be very loosely defined. Since it is the individual who suffers, surely it must be for the individual to decide when suffering has become "unbearable".

Stretching the categories of eligibility seems almost inevitable given that individuals have different thresholds of tolerance when it comes to suffering. It is not difficult to imagine that these categories might easily enough be extended to embrace the elderly, the infirm, and the cognitively impaired.[88]

Such fears might seem extravagant and unfounded. Biggar nevertheless draws a sombre conclusion from the analysis and warns that there are good reasons for caution when making assumptions about the inherent strength and stability of human society:

> The critics of the traditional moral and legal prohibition of such killing display a complacency about the security of human and liberal values that the history of the twentieth century does not warrant.[89]

A pre-eminent example of that history which ought to serve as a warning is the Nazi program of enforced euthanasia for the mentally ill and the disabled. Far from being a sudden and inexplicable outbreak of evil, the program was introduced gradually in 1938 and then accelerated early in 1939.

Hitler acted with prudence, notes Saul Friedländer, a historian of the Holocaust, because he did not want to provoke opposition from the churches without first testing the opinions of Catholic and Protestant leaders. When those opinions were sought, Friedländer remarks, "no opposition was voiced by any of the German clerics contacted by Hitler's Chancellery. The pope's delegate, too, remained silent."[90]

Small steps taken in Nazi Germany at first marked a change in the attitudes of the medical profession. These were fed by the regime's ideological commitment to pursuit of racial health — including by means other than euthanasia — and the idea that there are some lives not worth living.

This change in Germany's ethical sensibility was gradual and reached the point where it was deemed morally right to kill those who were considered worthless, or burdensome, or evil. Biggar noted Peter Haas's observation that the lesson to be learned from the Holocaust is "that people's moral inhibitions are easier to overcome than we might hope."[91]

The situation in Nazi Germany in the 1930s and debate about voluntary assisted suicide in 21st century Australia are, it needs to be stressed, completely distinct. Whereas the Nazis pursued notions of racial health and purity by means of non-voluntary euthanasia, contemporary proponents of assisted suicide say they are motived by compassion and concern for the welfare of the individual.

But we need to ensure that compassion for the infirm does not erode social and communal solidarity with the weak and the elderly. Likewise, we must not be blind to the threat that intense individualism, and its commitment to the moral superiority of individual rights, poses for the health of the social and cultural fabric.

Evidence from jurisdictions that have legalised assisted suicide and voluntary euthanasia does not yet appear to indicate that relaxing the law on killing human beings has propelled those societies down the slippery slope of moral degradation. But there are reasonable grounds for doubting that the prescribed circumstances in which the life of another person can already be taken will not expand. In the long run, it is also reasonable to suppose that expansion of categories of eligibility will pose a substantial threat to the health of human society.

Esteem for the value of human life, together with a humane commitment to the duty of showing compassion to the weak and alleviating the suffering of the vulnerable, are foundational moral components of our society. Changing the law to permit the killing of another person, for whatever reason, is an act of enormous moral significance. Once introduced, such a change will erode other moral principles as the justification for killing in one set of circumstances becomes, in time, the justification for killing in another.[92]

QUESTION 7

What impact will legalised assisted suicide have on the medical profession?

A fundamental tenet of medicine is that doctors are to heal and not to harm. It is a tenet expressed in the Hippocratic Oath, taken in times past by doctors and considered to set, in general terms, the limits and scope of the practice of medicine.

The tenet not to harm means that, when faced with an existing medical problem, it may be better for the physician to do nothing than to risk causing the patient harm. This is the principle of non-maleficence. At the root of that principle is the phrase, "First do no harm" (*Primum non nocere*).[93] But for some doctors, the practice of physician-assisted suicide is a direct violation of that tenet.[94]

Proponents of physician-assisted suicide — who do, of course, include doctors — often respond that helping someone to die who actively *wishes* to die can amount to an act of healing, and that death needs to be understood as a *benefit* to the patient. And sometimes, it may, indeed, be an act of compassion on the part of the doctor to help a patient die quickly and painlessly.

But *if* there are some cases where assisted suicide *might* be justified, it does not follow that the law ought to be changed to allow death to be delivered in *all* cases where it is sought. Justification of a specific instance is no warrant for a general justification.

A prior concern, however, is whether the motive of compassion can ever justify extending the role of doctors beyond caring, curing, and healing, to include the act of killing.

Limits to the use of power exercised within the relationship between doctor and patient are essential for ensuring that the practice of medicine is always ethical. Ethical practice is so important because of the imbalance of power between doctor and patient.

A patient in need of healing is exposed both physically and emotionally to the doctor whose own vulnerabilities are never disclosed to the patient in pursuit of the goal of diagnosis and cure. The physician remains detached, and there is an asymmetry of exposure and communication. This is the moral framework within which medicine is practised and, as Leon Kass has remarked, it legitimates the acquisition and exercise of power by the physician.[95]

This, in turn, requires that the physician must, at all times, exercise prudence, judgment, and self-restraint in the course of seeking healing and wholeness for the patient. Yet proponents of physician-assisted suicide argue that healing and wholeness may be achieved by intentionally *killing* the patient.

Such an intentional act must be distinguished from prescription of a course of treatment intended to be of benefit to the patient — such as for the relief of great pain — but which may turn out to be lethal. It must also be distinguished from the decision to stop medical intervention and to allow nature to take its course, especially if this is a course of action requested by the patient.

In making the medical decision to alleviate pain or withdraw treatment, the doctor does not intend to kill the patient, even though death may follow because of that decision. This is very different from a decision to end the life of the patient and to *make* the patient dead.

The decision to kill a patient surely contradicts the fundamental tenets of medicine, for "to bring nothingness is incompatible with serving wholeness," as Kass has noted. "One cannot heal — or comfort — by making nil. The healer cannot annihilate if he is truly to heal."[96]

Proponents of assisted suicide appeal to the relief of an individual's immediate experience of suffering as the principal justification for giving doctors permission to kill patients. This appeal, in turn, is rooted in a conviction about the primacy of individual autonomy, the conviction that a patient is entitled to demand the lethal intervention of a doctor, and a utilitarian judgment that an action which eliminates suffering can be deemed ethical.

But neither the instinct of mercy nor of compassion, no matter how sincerely felt by the doctor, can be allowed to displace the primary commitment physicians make to the *ethical* practice of medicine.

If the law permits doctors to express mercy by acts of *mercy killing*, the relationship of trust between doctor and patient is bound to be affected and harmed. Once doctors are licensed to kill, there is a real danger that a patient's trust in the authenticity of a doctor's professional commitment to her well-being will almost certainly be undermined.

Damage to the relationship between doctor and patient will also damage the standing of the profession of medicine; this, in turn, will inflict damage on the wider society.

Medicine is one of the few remaining social institutions around which there is a broad consensus about standards of morality, ethical practice, and trust. Commitment to this consensus about the practice of medicine transcends differences of class, ethnicity, and economic status forming what Margaret Somerville has described as "the existential glue that holds society together."[97]

Great harm will be caused to the capacity of medicine to maintain this consensus were the practice of physician-assisted suicide — that is, to be clear, the practice of permitting physicians intentionally to kill patients – made legal. The impact of this harm is not to be underestimated, as Somerville has remarked:

> It is a very important part of the art of medicine to sense and respect the mystery of life and death, to hold this mystery in trust, and to hand it on to future generations — especially future generations of physicians. We need to consider deeply whether legalizing euthanasia would threaten this art, this trust, and this legacy.[98]

Death is mysterious and very difficult to conceptualise for none of us can have any experience of that which is the complete *cessation* of experience, feeling, and thought.

The danger is that instead of viewing death as the inevitable end to life, medicine now views death as a form of failure of treatment. But human finitude is neither a moral nor medical failure; it is the boundary beyond which we cannot see, but beyond which we must pass.

Perhaps pleas for the legalisation of medical assistance in dying — whether by suicide or by voluntary euthanasia — are best understood as a last, desperate bid for autonomy in the face of that beyond which all notions of autonomy cease to be meaningful. But this is little less than what one writer has described as "self-determination run amok."[99]

It is not for medicine to ease the existential burden we each face of having to come to terms with human finitude and the inevitability of decay and death. The great and ancient art of medicine has no answer to the riddle of life.

THREESCORE YEARS AND TEN

Standing firm against autonomy absolutists

In mid-August 2018, one week before the Australian Senate debated – and subsequently voted down – Senator Leyonhjelm's bill to confer legislative territory rights, news broke that lethal injections had been given to three children in Belgium between January 2016 and December 2017. The children were aged 17, 11, and 9 – the latter two being the first cases of euthanasia administered to a child under the age of 12.[100]

Belgium, a country with one of the most liberal approaches to assisted dying, amended its law on euthanasia on 2 March 2014. The revised law authorises physicians to kill a child of any age who requests death (although parents can countermand that request).[101] Belgian doctors have now taken the step from providing assistance with suicide for the terminally ill, to killing deliberately a person whose life is simply deemed not worth living — and they are the first (as far as we know) to have killed children.

Proponents of euthanasia in Belgium insist that children are individuals who have the same capacity for making decisions as adults. Denying children the freedom to choose euthanasia because of an arbitrary age limit is, they say, discriminatory. In Belgium, any qualms about protecting the vulnerable young have been set aside in what one critic has described as "a kind of libertarian technocracy."[102] Even now that children are put to death, support for euthanasia remains undiminished in Belgium.

And in the Netherlands – which also has a very permissive euthanasia law – it is not just popular support that remains strong. Demand for euthanasia is rising sharply with figures showing an eight per cent increase in euthanasia and assisted suicide in 2017.

In that year, the annual report of the Regionale Toetsingscommissie Euthanasie – (Regional Euthanasia Review Committees, or RTE) – which provides an annual analysis of all deaths by euthanasia in the Netherlands, recorded 6,585 deaths. In 2020, the RTE recorded 6,938 deaths by euthanasia for that year – just over four per cent of all deaths in that country. This compares with 1,882 recorded deaths by euthanasia in 2002 when the Netherlands became the first country in Europe to legalise the practice.[103]

Euthanasia, with parental approval, is already available in the Netherlands for children aged between 12 and 15 years of age. In October 2020, the Dutch government outlined plans to extend availability of euthanasia to children between 1 and 12 years of age.[104]

Developments such as these prompted a stark warning from Theo Boer, a Dutch bioethicist, who initially supported legalisation of euthanasia in the Netherlands:

> Supply has created demand. We're getting used to euthanasia. We're no longer speaking about the exceptional situations that the law was created for, but a gradual process towards organised death. A border is being crossed between individual empathy and societal acceptance. A culture of euthanasia undermines our capacity to deal with suffering, and that is very bad for society.[105]

Just such a culture of euthanasia now threatens to take hold in Australia where public support for assisted dying remains strong. A Newspoll conducted for *The Australian* in August 2018, for example, found that 79 per cent of those surveyed were in favour of amending the law to allow physician-assisted suicide. Only 15 per cent were opposed.[106] Yet granting legal and moral permission to Australians wanting to end their lives will almost certainly lead to growth in demand for voluntary euthanasia.

Furthermore, evidence from jurisdictions where euthanasia and assisted suicide are lawful clearly indicates that the confidence Australians have in proposed legal constraints intended to regulate practice is misplaced. Once euthanasia is made available to certain specified categories of "suffering" people, demand for wider availability of euthanasia and assisted suicide will certainly grow.

That is because suffering is an ungovernable criterion. An individual's claim to be experiencing unendurable suffering will be hard to contest because such a claim is an entirely subjective judgment.[107] The categories of suffering are bound to expand beyond "terminal illness" as increasing numbers of people seek – and demand – relief from the suffering they claim to be experiencing by means of assisted suicide.

This demand for relief will be based on aggressive claims about rights. But, as this book has argued, "rights" involve obligations owed by, and to, individuals. Acknowledgement of the many responsibilities those mutual obligations place upon us is a determining factor in the health of civil society.

The absolutist claim to autonomy sits uneasily with the basic principles and requirements of civil society because a deliberate and voluntary act of suicide, whether with assistance or by euthanasia, amounts to a repudiation of those mutual obligations and their associated responsibilities. We do bear a general duty to relieve the suffering of others — but not at any such price demanded by the autonomy absolutists. As the psychiatrist and writer Anthony Daniels has observed:

> Once it becomes a question of rights rather than humanity, there is a kind of creep: why should the dying have all the best deaths? And who better than a person himself to decide whether his suffering is intolerable?[108]

Demands for legalisation of assisted suicide and euthanasia in Australia amount to a one-way ratchet effect in asserting the primacy of autonomy. But these demands need to be resisted because of the impact such autonomous choices will have on the wider society — on the family, on friends, on the local community — in which we live.

We must also resist arguments made by proponents of euthanasia that none of these considerations can ever outweigh the supposed primacy of individual choice; indeed, it is these very considerations that must override assertions of individual autonomy.

The span of human life is short, and death is certain. It is up to each of us to decide how we use the biblically allotted "threescore years and ten", but we have a limited number of years in which to make something of ourselves and to create lives that express meaning and purpose.

As Margaret Somerville has observed, people on both sides of the debate are well intentioned and believe they are fighting for the greater good in pursuit of that meaning and purpose. But there is disagreement about just what that greater good is.

> None of us on either side wants to see people suffer and the euthanasia debate is not about *if we will die* – we all will at some point. The debate is about *how we will die* and whether some ways of dying, namely euthanasia, are unethical and dangerous, especially to vulnerable and fragile people, and destructive of important shared values on which we base our societies.[109]

The legalisation of assisted suicide and euthanasia in Australia will enshrine in law a rejection of the duties we owe to others and of the claims others have upon us. As such, it poses a threat to the social, legal, and cultural norms underlying civil society in Australia.

This moral assault upon the dignity of every human being must be withstood and defeated.

Acknowledgements

The unexpected death by assisted suicide in 2016 of John Hirst, the distinguished Australian historian, sharpened my thinking about euthanasia. He had planned his death with assistance from a prominent pro-euthanasia campaign group, and had discussed openly his association with that group.

The impact of his death on family, friends, and his wider circle, however, was traumatic because John had kept details about the execution of his plan – including the timing – to himself. Observing reactions to John's death, I began to wonder how proponents of euthanasia and assisted dying could possibly describe the ending of his life as "dying with dignity". I am grateful to have had the chance to think about this question more critically in the course of many conversations I have had about euthanasia and assisted suicide.

This book is intended as a secular contribution to the debate about legalising euthanasia, and has been written as part of my work in the *Culture, Prosperity & Civil Society* program at the Centre for Independent Studies. I am grateful to Tom Switzer, the Executive Director of CIS, who has been a great advocate for the program.

Some of the ideas dealt with here were initially explored in "The Myth of the Right to Die", an article published in

Quadrant in July-August 2016, which I wrote in response to John's death. My thanks go to Anthony Cappello, at Connor Court, who gave me the opportunity to develop those ideas here.

I am also grateful to Patrick Parkinson who wrote the foreword to the first edition of the book and has provided a revised foreword for this edition. I am indebted, once again, to John Nethercote who has edited this revised edition with his customary care. The responsibility for any errors that remain is, as usual, entirely mine.

Peter Kurti
Sydney
8 November 2021

References

1. Emile Durkheim, *On Suicide*, (London: Penguin, 2006), 142.
2. "It's Official: Australians support assisted dying or euthanasia", *Roy Morgan* 10 November 2017) Australians support assisted dying or euthanasia - Roy Morgan Research
3. Margaret Somerville is Professor of Bioethics at University of Notre Dame Australia. She was previously Samuel Gale Professor of Law at McGill University.
4. Margaret Somerville, "Good ethics depends on good facts – but euthanasia debates are full of distortions and omissions", *MercatorNet*, (27 October 2021) https://mercatornet.com/good-ethics-depends-on-good-facts-but-euthanasia-debates-are-full-of-distortions-and-omissions/75489/
5. Alex Greenwich MP, "Voluntary Assisted Dying Bill 2021, Second Reading Speech", (14 October 2021) Voluntary Assisted Dying Bill 2021, Second Reading Speech - Alex Greenwich
6. For example, section 9 of the *Voluntary Assisted Dying Act* 2017 (Victoria) establishes certain eligibility criteria for accessing voluntary assisted dying that include diagnosis with an incurable and terminal disease which is expected to cause death within six months, and which is causing unrelievable suffering. http://www.legislation.vic.gov.au/Domino/Web_Notes/LDMS/PubStatbook.nsf/f932b66241ecf1b7ca256e92000e23be/B320E209775D253C-CA2581ED00114C60/$FILE/17-061aa%20authorised.pdf
7. Charlotte Hamlyn and Briana Shepherd, "David Goodall ends his life at 104 with a final powerful statement on euthanasia", *ABC News* (11 May 2018) http://www.abc.net.au/news/2018-05-10/david-goodall-ends-life-in-a-powerful-statement-on-euthanasia/9742528
8. Philip Nitschke is an Australian humanist, former physician, and founder of the pro-euthanasia group Exit International.
9. Charlotte Hamlyn and Briana Shepherd, "David Goodall ends his life", as above.

10 See Michael Cook, "The dangerous ideology of 'rational suicide'", *MercatorNet*, (11 May 2018) https://www.mercatornet.com/careful/view/the-dangerous-ideology-of-rational-suicide/21303

11 "David Goodall dies in Switzerland", *e-Deliverance*, (May-July 2018), https://exitinternational.net/deliverance/eDeliv-July-2018.pdf

12 Andrew Denton is an Australian television producer and pro-euthanasia advocate.

13 The question about religion in the 2016 ABS census was optional. Of those who responded, the percentage of Australians reporting "No religion" continued to increase – from 25 per cent in 2011, to 30 per cent. The percentage of those claiming a religious affiliation had declined from 68 per cent in 2011, to 60 per cent. While the proportion of Christians had declined from 88 per cent fifty years ago to just over 50 per cent, Australia has a number of other significant religious communities. Of those respondents who claimed a religious allegiance, 52 percent identified with Christianity, 3 per cent with Islam, and 2 per cent with Buddhism. The fastest growing religious group are Sikhs who have grown by 74 percent since 2011. Australian Bureau of Statistics, "2016 Census: Religion", http://www.abs.gov.au/AUSSTATS/abs@.nsf/mediareleasesbyReleaseDate/7E65A144540551D7CA258148000E2B85?OpenDocument

14 The following definitions have been adopted from Nigel Biggar, *Aiming to Kill: The Ethics of Suicide and Euthanasia*, (London: Darton, Longman and Todd: 2004) ix.

15 *Oxford English Dictionary*, (online edition) http://www.oed.com.ezproxy.csu.edu.au/view/Entry/65140?redirectedFrom=euthanasia#eid

16 https://exitinternational.net/about-exit/our-philosophy/

17 https://dwdnsw.org.au/your-rights/terminology/

18 Australian Bureau of Statistics, *Causes of Death, Australia* Causes of Death, Australia, 2020 | Australian Bureau of Statistics (abs.gov.au)

19 For a detailed account of deaths by self-harm in Australia, see Australian Institute of Health and Welfare, *Suicide & self-harm monitoring* Deaths by suicide over time - Australian Institute of Health and Welfare (aihw.gov.au)

References

20 Melissa Davey, "Highest Australian suicide rate in 13 years driven by men aged 40 to 44", *The Guardian* (9 March 2016). Figures in this section are also drawn from *Facts and stats about suicide in Australia* published by www.mindframe-media.info at http://www.mindframe-media.info/for-media/reporting-suicide/facts-and-stats

21 See *Statistics on Suicide* provided by Lifeline Australia https://www.lifeline.org.au/about-lifeline/lifeline-information/statistics-on-suicide-in-australia

22 The *Criminal Code Amendment (Suicide Related Material Offences) Act* 2005.

23 See, for example, the decision of the NSW Criminal Court of Appeal in *Justins v Regina* [2010] NSWCCA 242 (28 October 2010) http://www8.austlii.edu.au/cgi-bin/viewdoc/au/cases/nsw/NSWCCA/2010/242.html

24 The *Voluntary Assisted Dying Act* 2017 (Victoria) Section 9 (1) (d) (iv). http://www.legislation.vic.gov.au/Domino/Web_Notes/LDMS/PubStatbook.nsf/f932b66241ecf1b7ca256e92000e23be/B320E209775D253CCA2581ED00114C60/$FILE/17-061aa%20authorised.pdf. See also, Jean Edwards, "Euthanasia: Victoria becomes the first Australian state to legalist voluntary assisted dying", *ABC* News (29 November 2017) http://www.abc.net.au/news/2017-11-29/euthanasia-passes-parliament-in-victoria/9205472

25 Voluntary Assisted Dying Review Board, *Report of operations: January to June 2021*, (17 August 2021), 3.

26 For a comprehensive overview of the current laws relating to voluntary assisted dying and euthanasia in Australia, see "Voluntary Assisted Dying and Euthanasia", *End of Life Law in Australia*, *QUT*, (5 October 2021) QUT - Voluntary Assisted Dying and Euthanasia

27 Voluntary Assisted Dying Review Board, *Report of operations: January to June 2021*, as above.

28 "Euthanasia debate: NSW Parliament rejects bill on voluntary assisted dying", *ABC News* (17 November 2017).

29 *Voluntary Assisted Dying Bill 2021* (NSW) introduced by Mr A H Greenwich, MP Voluntary Assisted Dying Bill 2021 (nsw.gov.au)

30 Stephen Rice, "Vote on NSW assisted dying Bill delayed", *The Australian* (19 October 2021) Vote on NSW assisted dying Bill delayed (theaustralian.com.au)

31   David Leyonhjelm is a Senator for New South Wales, representing the Liberal Democratic Party.

32   Senator David Leyonhjelm, Second Reading Speech (3 March 2016). http://parlinfo.aph.gov.au/parlInfo/search/display/display.w3p;db=CHAMBER;id=chamber%2Fhansards%2F4338c56a-c77a-4a12-a868-652df075a3e9%2F0160;query=Id%3A%22chamber%2Fhansards%2F4338c56a-c77a-4a12-a868-652-df075a3e9%2F0157%22

33   Senator David Leyonhjelm, as above.

34   Amanda Vanstone, "Can't we just be decent to people at the end of their lives?", *Sydney Morning Herald* (1 July 2018) https://www.smh.com.au/politics/federal/can-t-we-just-be-decent-to-people-at-the-end-of-their-lives-20180629-p4zok5.html

35   "Federal Budget: Suicide Prevention Australia welcomes investment in wellbeing of older Australians", *Suicide Prevention Australia* (8 May 2018) https://www.suicidepreventionaust.org/news/federal-budget-suicide-prevention-australia-welcomes-investment-wellbeing-older-australians

36   http://christiansforve.org.au/public-opinion/ See also, for example, Andrew Dutney, "Christian support for voluntary euthanasia", *Monash Bioethics Review*, (April 1997), Vol. 16, No. 2, 15-22.

37   "One door closes, another opens", *The Economist* (19 September 2015).

38   *Oxford English Dictionary*, (online edition) http://www.oed.com.ezproxy.csu.edu.au/view/Entry/52653?redirectedFrom=dignity#eid

39   Margaret Somerville, *Death Talk: The Case Against Euthanasia and Physician-Assisted Suicide*, 2nd edition, (Montreal: McGill-Queen's University Press, 2014), xxviii.

40   Christopher M. Coope, "Death with Dignity", *Hastings Center Report*, Vol. 27, No. 5 (Sept. – Oct., 1997), 37-38, 37.

41   J. Donald Boudreau and Margaret Somerville, "Euthanasia is not medical treatment", *British Medical Bulletin* (2013), 106; 45-66, 60.

42   Boudreau, J.D., and Somerville, M., as above, 60

43   Yale Kamisar is Clarence Darrow Distinguished University Professor of Law Emeritus and Professor Emeritus of Law at the University of Michigan Law School.

References

44 Yale Kamisar, "The reasons so many people support physician-assisted suicide – and why these reasons are not convincing", *Issues in Law and Medicine*, 12.2 (Fall 1996), 113-131.

45 The *Oregon Death with Dignity Act* 2017 Data Summary, (Oregon Health Authority: Public Health Division, 2020), year23.pdf (oregon.gov)

46 Kevin Yuill lectures in History at the University of Sunderland, UK, specializing in the intellectual history of the twentieth century. He has written extensively on euthanasia.

47 Kevin Yuill, *Assisted Suicide: The Liberal, Humanist Case Against Legalization*, (Basingstoke, UK: Palgrave Macmillan, 2013), 43. Kindle edition.

48 *Julius Caesar*, II, ii.

49 Leon R. Kass, "Averting One's Eyes, or Facing the Music?: On Dignity in Death", *Hastings Center Studies*, Vol. 2, No. 2, *Facing Death* (May 1974), 67-80, 70.

50 See H. M. Chochinov, *Dignity Therapy*, (Oxford: OUP, 2012).

51 See further, Peter Kurti, *Sacred & Profane: Faith and belief in a secular society*, (Redland Bay QLD: Connor Court, 2020), 137-8. I am grateful to an anonymous referee for drawing *Dignity Therapy* to my attention, and for referring me to M. Somerville, "Dr Harvey's must-read book unpacks what dignity means", *Catholic Weekly*, (8 June 2017).

52 *Oxford English Dictionary* (online edition), http://www.oed.com.ezproxy.csu.edu.au/view/Entry/13500?redirectedFrom=autonomy#eid

53 Kevin Yuill, as above, 52.

54 Kevin Yuill, as above, 53.

55 John Safranek is a philosopher who writes about legal and political philosophy.

56 John P. Safranek, "Autonomy and Assisted Suicide: The Execution of Freedom", *Hastings Centre Report*, Vol. 28, No. 4, (Jul. – Aug., 1998), 32-36, 34.

57 Penny Lewis, "Rights Discourse and Assisted Suicide", *American Journal of Law & Medicine*, Vol. 27 (2001), 45-99, 77.

58 Penny Lewis, as above, 76.

59 Roger Scruton, *How To Be a Conservative*, (London: Bloomsbury, 2014), 75.

60 Leon Kass is an American physician, scientist, educator, and public intellectual.
61 Leon Kass, "Is There a Right to Die?", *Hastings Center Report* (January-February 1993), 42.
62 Daniel Callahan is an American philosopher who played a leading role in developing the field of biomedical ethics as co-founder of The Hastings Center.
63 Daniel Callahan, "When Self-Determination Runs Amok", *Hastings Center Report,* (April-March 1992) 52.
64 Daniel Callahan, as above, 52.
65 Daniel Callahan, as above, 53.
66 Neil Scolding, "Right to Die?", *Brain* (2011), 318-321, 320
67 *Oxford English Dictionary* (online edition), http://www.oed.com.ezproxy.csu.edu.au/view/Entry/193692
68 Source: Wikipedia, *Suicide legislation*, https://en.wikipedia.org/wiki/Suicide_legislation
69 Georgia Noon, "On Suicide", *Journal of the History of Ideas,* Vol. 39, No. 3, (July-Sept., 1978), 371-386, 372.
70 Quoted in Georgia Noon, as above, 374.
71 Sidney Hook was an American philosopher known for his contributions to the philosophy of history, the philosophy of education, political theory, and ethics.
72 Sidney Hook, "The Ethics of Suicide", *International Journal of Ethics*, Vol. 37, No.2, (Jan. 1927), 173-188, 174.
73 Sidney Hook, as above, 181.
74 Robert Talisse, "On Sidney Hook's 'The Ethics of Suicide'", *Ethics* 125, (January 2015), 549-551, 550.
75 See Kevin Yuill, as above, 107.
76 Kevin Yuill, as above, 107.
77 Leon Kass, "Is There a Right to Die?", as above, 43.
78 Leon Kass, as above, 37.
79 Charles Camosy, "Right to Die, or Duty to Die? The Slippery-Slope Argument against Euthanasia revisited", *ABC Religion & Ethics* (1 Sept. 2014), http://www.abc.net.au/religion/articles/2014/09/01/4078456.htm

80   See David A. Jones, "Is There a Logical Slippery Slope from Voluntary to Nonvoluntary Euthanasia?", *Kennedy Institute of Ethics Journal*, Vol. 21, No. 4, (2011), 379-404, 380.

81   John Keown is Professor Christian Ethics in the Kennedy Institute of Ethics at Georgetown University, Washington, DC.

82   See John Keown, *Euthanasia Examined: Ethical, Clinical and Legal Perspectives*, (Cambridge: CUP, 1995). See also, Henk Jochemsen and John Keown, "Voluntary euthanasia under control? Further empirical evidence from the Netherlands", *Journal of Medical Ethics* (1999), 25:16-21.

83   See Nigel Biggar, *Aiming to Kill: The Ethics of Suicide and Euthanasia*, (London: Darton, Longman and Todd, 2004), 129ff for a very detailed examination of the criticisms of Keown's study made by John Griffiths.

84   Nigel Biggar, as above, 142.

85   Nigel Biggar, as above, 157.

86   See *Oregon Death with Dignity Act* 2017 Data Summary, as above. Data sets for the entire period 1998-2020 are available at https://www.oregon.gov/oha/PH/PROVIDERPARTNERRESOURCES/EVALUATIONRESEARCH/DEATHWITHDIGNITYACT/Pages/ar-index.aspx

87   Charles Camosy, as above.

88   Nigel Biggar, as above, 145. For concerns about the collapse of safeguards in the Netherlands and the extension of euthanasia to those dementia and other mental illnesses, see also Michael Cook, "A Dutch euthanasia pioneer surveys the wreckage and despairs", *MercatorNet*, (20 June 2017) https://www.mercatornet.com/careful/view/a-dutch-euthanasia-pioneer-surveys-the-wreckage-and-despairs/19992

89   Nigel Biggar, as above, 158.

90   Saul Friedländer, *The Years of Persecution: Nazi Germany & The Jews 1933-1939*, (London: Phoenix, 1997), 210.

91   See Biggar, citing the work of Peter Haas, as above, 158.

92   For a concise but elegant discussion of the slippery slope, or "wedge" argument, see Paul Ramsey, "The Wedge: Not So Simple", *The Hastings Center Report*, Vol. 1, No. 3, (Dec., 1971), 11-12.

93 *Primum non nocere* is often thought to come from the Hippocratic Oath, historically taken by doctors, and one of the best known Greek medical texts. Although the Oath does include the promise "to abstain from doing harm", it does not include the phrase *primum non nocere* in that precise form. The Hippocratic Oath has been superseded by more extensive codes of medical ethics issued by national medical associations, including the Australian Medical Association. See https://ama.com.au/advocacy/ethics-professionalism

94 See, for example, Michael Cook, "American Medical Association stands firm on assisted suicide", *MercatorNet* (15 May 2018) https://www.mercatornet.com/careful/view/american-medical-association-stands-firm-on-assisted-suicide/21317

95 Leon R. Kass, "Neither for Love nor Money: Why Doctors Must Not Kill", *Public Interest*, Vol. 94 (1989: Winter, 25-45, 37.

96 Kass, "Neither for Love nor Money", as above, 41.

97 Margaret Somerville, *Death Talk: The Case Against Euthanasia and Physician-Assisted Suicide*, 2nd edition, (Montreal: McGill-Queen's University Press, 2014), 116.

98 Margaret Somerville, *Death Talk*, as above, 118.

99 Daniel Callahan, "When Self-Determination Runs Amok", as above, 55.

100 Charles Lane, "Children are being euthanized in Belgium", *Washington Post*, (6 August 2018) https://www.washingtonpost.com/opinions/children-are-being-euthanized-in-belgium/2018/08/06/9473bac2-9988-11e8-b60b-1c897f17e185_story.html?noredirect=on&utm_term=.75c7c7188ab7

101 See, for example, Barbara Miller, "Euthanasia law: Belgium passes legislation giving terminally ill children right to die", *ABC News*, (14 February 2014) https://www.abc.net.au/news/2014-02-14/belgium-child-euthanasia-law/5259314?nw=0&r=HtmlFragment#:~:text=Belgium%20has%20become%20the%20first,%2D44%2C%20with%2012%20abstaining

102 Charles Lane, as above.

103 Regional Euthanasia Review Committees Annual Report 2020 https://english.euthanasiecommissie.nl/the-committees/documents/publications/annual-reports/2002/annual-reports/annual-reports

References

104 "Letter to Parliament response to report on medical decisions concerning end-of-life children" [sic], *Rijksoverheid*, (13 October 2020) Letter to Parliament response to report on medical decisions concerning end-of-life children | Parliamentary | Rijksoverheid.nl

105 Harriet Sherwood, "A woman's final Facebook message before euthanasia: 'I'm ready for my trip now'", *The Guardian* (18 March 2018) https://www.theguardian.com/society/2018/mar/17/assisted-dying-euthanasia-netherlands. See also, Theo A. Boer, "Recurring themes in the debate about euthanasia and assisted suicide", *Journal of Religious Ethics*, (2007), 35.5:529-555.

106 For discussion of the Newspoll results, see Simon Benson and Greg Brown, "Threat to Malcolm Turnbull as euthanasia cabinet split looms", *The Australian* (14 August 2018) https://www.theaustralian.com.au/national-affairs/threat-to-malcolm-turnbull-as-euthanasia-cabinet-split-looms/news-story/9e292387c2a1e-a790175e88c81f297b8

107 See, for example, Zed Seselja, "Why I'm voting 'no' on the assisted suicide bill: Seselja", *Sydney Morning Herald*, (13 August 2018) https://www.smh.com.au/politics/federal/why-i-m-voting-no-on-the-assisted-suicide-bill-seselja-20180813-p4zx94.html

108 Anthony Daniels, private correspondence with the author (2 June 2016).

109 Margaret Somerville, "We need to develop an anti-euthanasia vaccine – at warp speed", *Mercatornet*, (25 October 2021) We need to develop an anti-euthanasia vaccine – at warp speed » MercatorNet

Euthanasia